TABLE OF

I

ACKNOWLEDGMENTS

The following list of persons talked with me, wrote a reflection, commented on a chapter, donated pictures, provided information or moral support, and/or technical assistance. I thank each of you for your input. I could not have done it without you. "TO GOD BE THE GLORY"

Mr. Abraham Aduwera
Mrs. Dorothy Shavers Brown
Pastor Matthew Southall Brown, Sr.
Rev. Matthew Southall Brown, Jr.
Dr. Lorene Brown
Mrs. Lottie W. Brown
Mr. Robert Brown
Ms. Sheila Bussey
Mr. Albert Benjamin Cameron
Mr. Terrell Closs
Ms. Geraldine Dawson
Mrs. Joia Ellis Dinkins
Dr. Patricia Dugas
Dr. Gerald L. Durley
Rev. Edward Ellis, Jr.
Mrs. Lillian Williams Ellis
Mr. and Mrs. Robert Glover
Mr. and Mrs. James Griffin
Mrs. Sara Derrick Herring
Mrs. Carmilita Cureton Hopkins
Ms. Michelle Hunter
Mr. Eddie Lamar Jones, Jr.
Mrs. Lauretta Williams Jones
Mrs. Maxine Brown Jones
Ms. Mary A. McPherson
Ms. Marion Butler Marshall
Mr. Joseph Miller
Mrs. Janet Milton
Ms. Francine W. Owens
Mrs. Ivy Paige Richardson
Ms. Brenda Roberts
Ms. Anita Singleton Prather
Dr. Loren Schweninger
Mrs. Helen Fletcher Scroggins
Mr. Ramel Spruill
Ms. Christa Brown Stephens
Mr. Kenneth Tucker
Mrs. Laura Derrick Webb

II

INTRODUCTION

INTRODUCTION

Growing up in Savannah, Georgia during the 1950s and 1960s made a lasting impression on my life. I say this because I grew up in three segregated communities—Liberty City, Sun Valley and Cann Park. This segregation, however, created clean, safe, and encouraging environments. As a child, I didn't realize these factors. As I reflect on these communities, I remember African Americans controlled businesses, churches, restaurants, recreational facilities, educational institutions, medical and pharmaceutical establishments. However, the recollection that has stayed in my mind were the well kept homes. We had neighborhoods anchored by homeowners that took pride in their property. They sacrificed, made and created neighborhoods, not 'hoods' or 'ghettoes.'

To me, my neighborhood was the foundation upon which families stood. It was a haven of encouragement which housed lawyers, doctors, pastors, teachers, and business owners. People of all social strata intermingled on the streets with ease and without fear. As a child of the Cann Park Community, I skated down the infamous 45th Street hill. I zoomed pass the homes of Dr. McDew, Dr. Wilson, and College Administrator Freeman. As the street leveled, I slowly coasted pass the homes of the Sessions, Delawares, Bedgoods, Sextons, and DeLongs. Whizzing down 39th Street on my bicycle, I passed the homes of Richard and Emma Williams of First Bryan Baptist Church, Mrs. Ella P. Law— famed teacher of the Language Arts at A. E. Beach High School, business owner Charles Allen and School Administrator Erma Fields.

Traveling to George W. DeRenne Elementary, in my formative years, I rode in my parents' blue 1955 Plymouth. We passed the mansion of Dr. and Mrs. Henry Collier on Liberty Parkway. I visited my relatives at Derrick's Inn, a 23 acres recreational site purchased by Joseph and Mamie Derrick in 1923. The family's home, a stately green structure, stood on this property. Joseph Miller, a cousin of mine who spent his adolescent years here, stated, "An indelible impression was made on my consciousness, in this house. My first thought of attending Massachusetts Institute of Technology (MIT) was born in this place."

True inspiration came as I drove to Thunderbolt, Georgia, traveling to Savannah State College, as a young student. On Whatley Avenue, College Street and the surrounding side-streets, I marveled at the homes of the college administrators, professionals and college teachers: Robinson, Blake, Jones, Brock, Lumpkin, Alexis, Butler, Kelson, Blalock, Thorpe, Williams, Bryant, Hill and Owens.

A magical place that reflected safety and security was the Wormsloe Plantation. Every first Sunday my father, Rev. Matthew Southall Brown, Sr., a deacon at First African Baptist Church, would commune Mr. Jenkins who lived on the Plantation. As we entered the Plantation, an old White couple, weathered by time, was the gatekeeper. After sounding the horn of our 1955 blue Plymouth, an aged White man would open the gate. A picturesque dirt road lay in front of us, lined with neatly trimmed oak trees. Once we reached our destination, Mr. Jenkins' home, I remember seeing a stately African-American gentleman dressed in his Sunday's finest waiting to partake of the Lord's Supper—Communion. The most striking memory I have was his modestly furnished wooden home, probably an old slave cabin. My siblings—Maxine, Christa, and Matthew— and I were placed in a room filled with toys to occupy our time. As the short communion service came to an end, we loaded back into the car, headed to another home. However, there was another home on Wormsloe that was seen just above the neatly trimmed hedges. It was a white columned antebellum home. As children we often inquired as to why we couldn't visit this home. An answer was never given by our parents.

Wheaton Street was a place of inspiration and motivation. On this street my father sat on the porches of two great women seeking insight and wisdom. Mrs. Pearl E. Smith and Mrs. Sweet Bing Roberts were two outstanding educators whose homes we visited. Sunday afternoons we visited their homes that were perched on a hill, slightly angled, with two stories and very neatly kept white rocking chairs waiting to be used. Across the street from these homes was the beautiful home of the Moores. These homes served as the backdrop for the topics that were discussed: education, religion, family, civil rights and politics. In the next block Clarence and Inez Brown's home stood trimmed in green; nestled on the corner. These were our relatives. I still have memories of the sunroom in this home filled with plants and flowers.

Ironically, Willie Brown, my grandfather's brother, was the first principal of Springfield Terrance School, which was later named Pearl S. Smith Elementary School. Helen Brown Fletcher and Helen Fletcher Scroggins (mother and daughter, respectively) were on the faculty of Pearl E. Smith, at the same time.

My grandparents, Helen and Christopher Brown, were masters at building, purchasing, financing, and maintaining homes. They owned three homes in Savannah, Georgia—519-521 Hartridge Street; 925 West Victory Drive, and 927 West Victory Drive. After the death of my grandfather, my grandmother built two homes: 2704 Stevens Street, Savannah, Georgia; and 212 Isaac Street, Columbia, South Carolina. What a legacy! Even though my grandmother's homes were showrooms, they reflected her inner strength and determination to complete a task.

The Geechee-Gullah Culture had a major influence on my

appreciation of homes beyond my community. On Hilton Head Island, South Carolina, African Americans from the island and Savannah owned homes, on segregated beaches. The names of these beaches were Collier, Bradley, Singleton, and Burke. I remember traveling to Bradley Beach with my parents; visiting the home of Mrs. Nancy H. Walker and her sister, Mrs. Stewart. They often gave us the privilege to use their home during the summer. The area contained the homes of prominent Savannahnians and South Carolinians. Some of the persons owning land and homes were Dr. and Mrs. Henry Collier, Mr. and Mrs. George Washington, and Mrs. Virginia Kiah. While researching Hilton Head land parcels in the Oceans and Coastal Resources Management (OCRM) Setback Zone, I came across a parcel of land belonging to Mrs. Virginia Kiah, on Singleton Beach. Dr. and Mrs. Kiah were well known educators in Savannah, Georgia. The Kiah's home/museum on West 36th Street housed many of Mrs. Kiah's paintings.

COMMUNITY is a photographic and reflective story that captures the essence of the African-American community, as seen through my eyes and the eyes of others. It is a journey through the streets of mostly west Savannah, postal code 31405. It is a journey that was pleasant in the late 1950s to the mid to late 1960s. Sadly, today the journey is painful, and not very safe. Where well kept homes once stood, now stand homes in ruin or in need of numerous repairs. Before I can't recognize the homes that anchored my community, this book, COMMUNITY, had to be written to preserve a sense of common history, and a sense of comm 'UNITY.'

The communities highlighted in this anthology were wealthy in terms of expectations, pride and dignity. Present and future generations of African-American young people must recognize how stable communities can in many ways create sustainable cities, states and nations.

"The strength of a nation derives from the integrity found within the wall of its homes."
—Confucius/Brown

III

VARIATIONS ON COMMUNITY

COMMUNITY

VARIATIONS ON THE TITLE

1. Somali .... Bulsho, Dad Meel Ku Wada Nool
2. Vietnamese .... Cong Dong
3. Spanish .... Comunidad
4. Swahili .... Harambee
5. French .... Comunite
6. Welsh .... Fy Nghymuned/Yn Gymraey
7. Arabic .... Ummah
8. Hebrew .... Kehilla
9. German .... Gemeinde or Kommune
10. Latin .... Communitas
11. Old English .... Gemaenscipe
12. Ebonics .... Hood
13. Dutch .... Gemeenschap

This work is a reflective glance of what COMMUNITY meant to me growing up in Savannah, Georgia. The absence of UNITY in some of our present communities is a sad commentary that must be remedied.

IV

TITLES

Titles considered for this book, COMMUNITY:
Progress In The Midst Of Oppression
1923-2015 Savannah, Georgia

1. A Look at Homes Built by African Americans in Savannah, GA
2. African American Homeownership: A Legacy of Pride
3. A Legacy of Pride: African American Homeownership
4. We Did It Ourselves: African American Homeownership
5. Savannah, Georgia: A Look into African American Homeownership
6. Builders of Our Past: African American Homeownership
7. A Firm Foundation: African American Homeownership
8. Laying Firm Foundations
9. Establishing Roots: The African-American Community in Savannah, Georgia
10. With Our Hands: Homeownership in the African American Community
11. We Built With Pride
12. Foundations
13. From the Roof Tops
14. From Houses to Homes
15. Where I Got My Start
16. Homes that Helped to Anchor the African American Communities
17. Doors: An Open Invitation to the Homes Owned by African Americans
18. Your Invitation to Homes Built by African Americans
19. Establishing Community: Homes Built by African Americans
20. From Neighborhoods to Hoods
21. They Once Existed
22. They Still Exist
23. Bricks and Mortar
24. Saving and Preserving the Foundations of the African American

V

GAITS OF AIMLESSNESS

GAITS OF AIMLESSNESS

"I ain't going back there after I graduate….and the ones who wanna go back don't actually wanna live there, they wanna help. I don't understand why they don't wanna go back but I believe you can never fully understand the people fighting in the war if you don't live in the trenches with them." This quotation was written by Gabriel Sheffield (G Sheff). He was writing his reactions to the book Disintegration: The Splintering of Black America, authored by Eugene Robinson. Mr. Sheffield is reflecting on his experiences growing up in inner-city Dallas, Texas. Sadly, he further remarks that he didn't remember knowing a single person in his neighborhood who was a doctor, lawyer, or college graduate. It took a trip to his father who lived in the suburbs and entering college for him to meet successful Black people.

In the September 17, 2010 edition of The Root, an article was written entitled "Montgomery, Alabama, Razing Homes of African Americans along the Civil Rights Trail," authored by Nsenga Burton. The article investigated the demolition of "blighted" homes. These homes are owned disproportionately by African Americans who are impoverished. Rosa Parks, a civil right icon, once lived along this federally funded Civil Rights Trail, the article states. In this article, David Beito, a history professor at the University of Alabama, is quoted as saying, "What's happening in Montgomery is a civil rights crisis." He further described this process as "eminent domain" through the back door. Finally, the author criticizes the government for not paying fair market value for these homes, and leaving the homeowners with the demolition bill.

An artist by the name of Ryan Mendoza purchased Rosa Parks' Detroit home after it was slated for demolition. In 2016 he took the house apart, and shipped the pieces to Berlin, Germany. He rebuilt it in six months. Earlier, Rosa Parks' niece, Rhea McCauley, purchased the home from the City Detroit for $500.00 and donated it to Mendoza. Mrs. McCauley stated, "It is something that is precious," as she visited the home in Germany. There is a Rosa Parks school as well as a Martin Luther King, Jr. School and kindergarten in Berlin. Mendoza hopes to sell the house to an institution, with the profits going to the Rosa Parks Foundation. If we forget, they will remember.

Additionally, the spring 2010 edition of The Southern Scene Magazine, featured two articles discussing the displacement of African Americans in Savannah, Georgia. The first article was entitled, "Reflections of Southern Black Communities: Past and Present." The second article was entitled, "The

Displacement of Blacks in Savannah." Both were written by Brenda Walker. The author focused on the gentrification and revitalization of the Savannah Historic District, which at one time was heavily populated by African Americans. Increasing property and insurance costs along with lost political clout are scenes being played out across inner cities in America.

These three disturbing accounts of the African American community today lead me to this question: What will become of the African-American community in Savannah, as I knew it, five decades from now? As I travel from Decatur, Georgia where I now reside, to my hometown of Savannah, Georgia, I have pondered this question for years. The vibrant African American community of my childhood creates in me a sense of fear and hopelessness. As I travel the streets of my childhood community, I see Gaits of Aimlessness—abandoned homes, and an aging population of original homeowners. Proudly displayed as one who has power and influence in my childhood community, a gangsta on My Space now represents my community. This overt display motivated me to document the Lamina Propria (foundation, scaffolding, adhesives) of my childhood African-American community who owned their homes, raised their children, nurtured other children in the community and provided for their families.

In Dr. Condoleeza Rice's memoir, A Memoir of Family: Extraordinary Ordinary People, she described her Birmingham, Alabama neighborhood as a "Placid Cocoon of family, church and school." Describing her extended family of grandparents, aunts, uncles and cousins, she saw them as providing the first layer of support and nurture. One of the most powerful descriptions she gave of her community in her memoir is as follows:

"The community mentors were not far outside the family circle, and our little neighborhood of Titusville provided a strong network of black professionals who were determined to prepare their kids for productive lives."

CommUNITY is my dedication to African American families who thought it not robbery to realize that the INTEGRITY OF THEIR COMMUNITY LAY WITHIN THE WALLS OF THEIR HOMES. After reading this work, one might surmise that my reflections are being done through rose colored lenses. That may be true. However, I remember being told as a young teacher that students might forget what you teach them. However, they will never forget how you made them feel. I will never forget how my community made me feel—safe, secure, free, hopeful, encouraged, motivated, and spiritually wealthy.

Below are some of the positive influences that framed my concept of what a community was in the late 1950s and 1960s:

1. Locally Black owned businesses: Rainey's Shoe Shop; Mrs. B's Convenience Store, Al's Cleaners, Beavers' Barbershop,; Bynes-Royall Funeral Home, Carver State Bank, Sam Stevens' Boat (The Waving Girl), Camilla Wells' Music Parlor;

2. Ms. Alice, the maid at A. E. Beach Junior High School, telling the students to "drag their feet," as they entered the building;

3. Rev. Matthew Southall Brown, Sr. (my father) leading the kids in the community on skating and biking rides during the Christmas Holidays;

4. Walking to 1014 West 41st Street to Deacon Edward Williams, Sr.'s (my grandfather) home to shine his shoes for Sunday services ($0.15 was the pay).

5. Mrs. Crawford supervising the daily activities at Cann Park;

6. Walking to A. E. Beach High School's Child Development Center, heading to Ms. Betty Dowse's kindergarten class, being escorted to school by Mrs. Lillian Williams Ellis (my aunt) and Toodalu;

7. Well kept homes of hard working African-American families;

8. Carrying meals prepared by my grandmother, Mrs. Helen Robinson Brown, to Mrs. Mabel Marks whose body was plagued with arthritis;

9. Sitting on the fourth pew facing the grand piano, scared to move or talk at First African Baptist Church;

10. The calm yet convincing voice of my mother (Mrs. Lottie Williams Brown) telling—not requesting—my siblings and me to be in the house when the street lights flickered;

11. Not seeing police cars patrolling our community.

Yes, my hindsight may be tainted, but it's tainted with strokes of love. Age and memory are blessings. What a wonderful feeling to reflect on my COMMUNITY with a sense of, "THEY CARED ABOUT US."

COMMUNITY seeks to recall the names of the men and women who taught the children of the COMMUNITY in ways they will never know.

VI

CUYLER-BROWNVILLE
(BROWNSVILLE)

"Yet With a Steady Beat"
Cuyler-Brownville (Brownsville) Community

Bordered by West Victory Drive, Martin Luther King, Jr. Drive (West Broad Street) and Stiles Avenue, this community is nestled. Still peppered with tree lined streets, stately two story homes and cozy bungalows, this community harbored some of Savannah's most prominent African-American families, educators, civic leaders and entrepreneurs.

Three signature historic sites are found in this community. Florance Street School was built in 1929. It served as an educational facility molding the minds of young African-American children. Charity Training Hospital, once known as McKane Hospital, began in 1896. Doctors Cornelius and Alice McKane began this hospital to train African-American nurses. I was born in this hospital on March 2, 1951. Laurel Grove South Cemetery opened in the year 1853.

Prominent members of Savannah's African-American community are buried at this location. Three outstanding church leaders are entombed here: Rev. Andrew Bryan of First Bryan Baptist Church, Rev. Evans Oliver Sylvester Cleveland of St. John Baptist Church and Rev. Henry Cunningham of Second African Baptist Church. The unmarked slave graves denote the status of our ancestors in Savannah. Miss. Lila Burns, my great aunt, purchased a plot so that members of her family could be entombed. Today you will see, carved into a five feet headstone, the members of the Burns and Brown families dating back to the late 1800s.

Socially and demographically this community has somewhat changed. Examining the statistics of the area, paints a very interesting picture.

Population   2,989
Area   .0386 Square Miles
Population Density   7,516 Square Miles
Percent Below Poverty Level 33.1%
Units with a Mortgage   37.8%
Married Couples with Children   23.3%
Single Mother Household   23.3%
Median Age   28.1

All isn't lost!! This community has a strong association of residents who care about their neighborhood. An advocate and voice for this community is the Cuyler-Brownville (Brownsville) Neighborhood Association Task Force and the Cuyler-Brownville (Brownsville) Youth Task Force.

"Yet with a steady beat," this community still thrives.

Reflections: Yamacraw, Yamacraw Village and West 41st Street
Lottie Williams Brown

I was born August 22, 1926 in Beaufort, South Carolina. My parents were Edward Williams, Sr. and Regina Dawson Williams. For the past 85 years I was under the impression that my birthday was August 4, 1926. However, after receiving a copy of my birth certificate, the date indicated August 22. Having been delivered by a midwife in rural Beaufort County, actual birth dates and the dates recorded for public record didn't always match.

I was told at the age of three months my family moved to Savannah, Georgia. Two of my siblings—Edward "Buck" Williams, Jr. and Isaac Williams—were born in Beaufort, South Carolina prior to our move to Savannah. We moved into an area called Yamacraw. Our home was on York Street. Three of my siblings—Lauretta Williams Jones, Isadore Williams and Lillian Williams Ellis—were born at this location.

Pilgrim Baptist Church was our family's house of worship. It was located in Yamacraw. Our pastors were Rev. Richard Simmons and Rev. J. J. Dinkins. My father chaired the Deacon Board of this church for 27 years. As children, we were very active in the church, along with my mother who sang in the choir.

In 1941 my family moved into Yamacraw Village. We were the third family to occupy our home. Our address was 522 Yamacraw Village. The development was very nice. Flowers were plentiful and the lawns were well kept. We knew our neighbors. It was a great place to experience as a child. Our home was behind First Bryan Baptist Church. As children we would peer into the windows of the church on Tuesday nights, listening to the fervent prayers and hymns of its members. Rev. Levi M. Terrell was the pastor of this church during my youth. My youngest brother, Isadore, was born at this location. My youngest sister, Lillian Williams Ellis, would later marry Rev. Edward Ellis, Jr., who served as the pastor of First Bryan Baptist Church for 26 years. "The Lord Moves in Mysterious Ways."

In Yamacraw Village, Eugene and Ida Bell Gadsden were residents. Mr. Gadsden was the director of Yamacraw Village. Mrs. Gadsden was my homeroom teacher. It was my responsibility to deliver Mrs. Gadsden's class work to the school when she was expecting her first child. Located on West Broad Street, the Scarborough House is found. As a young student, I attended West Broad Street Elementary School (The Scarborough House).

I remember the foundational families of Yamacraw Village. These families were: the Robinsons, Ledbetters, Gadsdens, Webbs, Williamses, Burns, Freemans and the Grants. Yamacraw Village was a community, a neighborhood and a family oriented place to live.

When my family's condition improved economically, we moved to 1014 West 41st Street. A cluster of homes were built by an African-American builder by the name of Mr. McKelvey. Our home stood in the middle of the block, surrounded by some of the finest neighbors you ever would want to meet. The McMillans, Kelsons, Blalocks, Pickneys, Gatrells, Shankses, Walkers, Cobbinses, Johnsons, Minuses, Cargos, Miss. Odessa and her mother were some of the neighbors I recall. These proud homeowners worked as nurses, teachers, hair stylists, truck drivers, insurance salesmen and housewives.

Unique to this period in history, the 1940s saw milk and ice deliveries to our homes. Annette Dairy delivered milk and juice on a specially built horse drawn wagon. The number of glass bottles you left on your front porch indicated the quantity of milk and juices you would receive. Mr. Byler delivered ice for our ice box. Covered with a brown canvass cloth, the block of ice was hauled to 1014 West 41st Street. The ice was processed at the ice house on Whitaker Street.

My family lived in this house long enough so that my children could experience the caring atmosphere created by Edward Williams and Regina Dawson Williams. It was at this home that my mother died at the young age of 52; leaving two young children behind—Lillian and Isadore. It was this home that helped to launch my relationship with my husband of 64 years, Pastor Matthew Southall Brown, Sr.

At this writing, the home stands vacant and void of the voices that nurtured its occupants. In the memories of the senior members of my family, the home is still occupied.

Yamacraw and Cuyler-Brownville (Brownsville) Communities
Lillian Sharon Williams Ellis

I entered the world on August 11, 1938. I was born to the parents Edward Williams and Regina Dawson Williams. My family resided on York Street at this time. Our home was between Fahm and West Broad Streets. In 1941, at the age of three, my family moved to Yamacraw in the village. We were the third family to assume residency there.

On December 7, 1941, the Japanese attacked Pearl Harbor, which brought the United States into World War II. I have vivid memories of men going to war. A neighbor, whose last name was Hardy enlisted in the Navy. He never returned; leaving six children fatherless. My brother, Edward Williams, Jr., whom we called Buck, enlisted in the Navy. Our oldest brother, Isaac (Ike), enlisted in the Maritime Marines. He was going to join without my father's (Papa) permission. Papa met Ike in the hallway early in the morning on the morning he was to enlist. He told Ike that a man in his dreams told him to tell Ike not to board the ship. The ship sank that night, killing everyone on board. During the war, I remember my father placing a blanket over the radio so that it would not reflect light. This was done because German u-boats were spotted off the east coast of the United States.

My education began at age five. I attended Hodge Memorial Kindergarten. My favorite things were tomato juice and playing the triangle at music time. After graduation from Hodge, I attended West Broad Street School (The Scarborough House) from grades first through third. Miss. Curley was my first grade teacher. Mrs. Maxwell was my second grade teacher, and Mrs. Williams was my third grade teacher. May Day and the May pole celebration at West Broad Street School stand out in my mind. During the second half of my third grade year, I rode to school with Mrs. Williams. That made me feel special. In the fourth grade I transferred to Florance Street School. Papa purchased our first house on West 41st Street. Mrs. Ala Mae Lovette was my teacher. She gave me the opportunity to sing my first solo in public. The song was entitled, "What Is America to Me?" I had been playing the piano since the first grade, and now I was singing as well. My parents enhanced this interest by enrolling me in piano, organ and theory lessons. My teachers were as follows: Mrs. Julia Legree (grades 1-3), and Mrs. Camilla Wells (grades 4-12). In those days w paid 50¢ for lessons.

At age eleven my mother died. This was traumatic. However, God sent an angel in the form of a neighbor, Marie Kelson, who was a licensed nurse. She taught me many practical lessons. Two of those lessons were how to drive and maintaining a checkbook. The greatest thing she did for me was to encourage me to attend Spelman College. While Marie worked in Atlanta, at Grady Hospital, she witnessed the poise and grace of young Spelman women. She wanted me to experience this college. First, I had to graduate from high school.

I attended Cuyler-Beach Junior High School. My class was the first in the school to take an algebra course. Rev. Willis Gwyn was my mathematics teacher. Rev. Gwyn died June 17, 2011. Mrs. Parker was my music teacher. She taught our choir the Hallelujah Chorus.

High school was a time of discovery and involvement. I participated in several extra curricula activities at A. E. Beach High School. Some of them were: The Honor Society, Tri-Hi-Y, and the chorus. In tenth grade, I was chosen as the class queen. In twelfth grade I was selected as Miss. Congeniality. My circle of friends consisted of Margaret Solomon, Arthur Hunter, Dandy Polite Taylor, Richardine Ralph, Donald Kennedy, and William Bush. I graduated in 1959, raking tenth in my class. There were 365 graduates. I was headed to Spelman.

I traveled to Spelman by train, on the Nancy Hanks. It was about a seven hour drive to Atlanta. Most students from Savannah attending Morehouse, Clark, and Atlanta University rode the Nancy Hanks. This was the first time I traveled without my parents. When I arrived at Spelman I was somewhat depressed over my mother's death. However, Spelman was the experience of a lifetime. I was exposed to some of the best teachers—who opened doors of learning for me. Dr. Howard Zinn, Dr. Grace Boggs, Dr. Joyce Johnson, Dr. Wendall Whalum, Dr. Willis-Lawrence James and Dr. Norman Rates were some of the examples. They were inspiring great teachers, and wonderful examples of excellence. They loved their profession and it affected my life forever.

At Spelman I was one of the lead soloists in the Spelman Glee Club. I sang with the Spelman-Morehouse-Atlanta University Chorus, the select Morehouse Chapel Choir, and Atlanta's Congregational Church Choir. I had the highest (vocal) range (C) of all soprano voices. My most memorable experience was singing at the Annual Christmas and Spring Concerts.

Upon my gradation from Spelman, I was hired as a music instructor in Monroe, Georgia. Little did I know that a young man, by the name of Edward Ellis, Jr., was observing me. Even though the Monroe community had assigned Mr. Ells a bride, he had his eyes on me. We were married August 11, 1962. From this union, three children were born—Sharon, Joia and Edward.

"The Lord moves in mysterious ways." As a young child I grew up behind historical First Bryan Baptist Church. Little did I know that my husband would become the pastor; and that I would become the First Lady of that church. We served First Bryan Baptist and the Savannah community for 26 years. I have come full circle.

Aunt Lauretta Williams Jones
Memorial Service
Savannah, Georgia
Leonard Brown
July 25, 2015

There was a time in the African-American community when family members knew their relatives, lived in the vicinity of their relatives and visited their relatives. Parents made sure their children knew their relatives.

When my family lived in Liberty City, our cousins lived on the same street. When we lived on Cathy Street, our uncle lived down the street. When we lived on Victory Drive, our grandfather lived on 41st Street. Our grandmother lived behind us and my aunt lived on 47th Street. Even though Aunt Lillian and Uncle Edward once lived in Monroe, Georgia, they made trips to Savannah; bringing their children. We traveled to

Derrick's Inn to visit our great-aunt and uncle, Mamie and Joe, and our cousins.

Aunt Lauretta lived in New York City, and made it a point to visit her family in Savannah. Once a year our family would travel to the train station in the summer, where we waited for one or two trains arriving from the north, The Silver Star or the Silver Median.

When the gigantic engines pulled into the station and came to a halt, the conductor would place two or three pieces of blue Samsonite luggage—trimmed in beige—on the ramp. From the segregated silver car would step Aunt Lauretta—dressed to the nines. When she recognized us she would say, "You Look Fabulous." When her visit ended, her parting words would be, "Continue To Do Well."

Finally, I consider Aunt Lauretta to be the Rosa Parks of our family. The story is that, while working in Estill, South Carolina, she and a friend went into a store to purchase a dress. Aunt Lauretta wanted to try the dress on. The white clerk said she couldn't. Aunt Lauretta tried it on anyway. She was fired from her job as a Home Economics teacher. She moved to New York. Many years later, I met her principal, Mr. Bates, in Greenville, South Carolina where I was employed.

Thank you, Aunt Lauretta, for all you did for Bryon, your family and friends.

Charity Hospital and Training School for Nurses

This was the site of the first hospital in Savannah to train African-American doctors and nurses. Named for Doctors Cornelius and Alice McKane, it began on June 1, 1896, when a small group of African Americans received a charter to operate the McKane Hospital for Women and Children and Training School for Nurses. The original hospital was a five-room wooden building. Charity Hospital completed this brick structure in 1931 and continued here until 1964. The building was used as a nursing home until 1976 and was rehabilitated for housing in 2002.

Erected by the Georgia Historical Society,
Mercy Housing SouthEast, Sisters of Mercy,

VII

CANN PARK

In Search of Mrs. Crawford
Cann Park

A water fountain that never stopped running greeted breathless children as they ran from their homes to Cann Park. Surrounded by 45th, 46th, Stevens, and Bullock Streets, Cann Park can still be found. It is a place that conjures up memories that are quite pleasant. [It is a place that conjures up pleasant memories.] Anchoring this park were families that kept their watchful eyes on the happenings taking place on and around the park. The Delawares, Bedgoods, Sweeneys, Jacksons, Sessions, Gibbses, Cargos, Maynards, Warricks, Jameses, Sextons, and DeLongs were examples of some of the foundational families.

Gone are the days when Mrs. Crawford, the park director, monitored the activities of the children. She issued the playground equipment for the games to be played that day. A green wooden chest with a rickety lock housed these items: sand bags, baseball bats, dodge balls, baseballs, horseshoes, basketballs, and baseball gloves. Mrs. Crawford, who lived on 44th Street, was a fixture of the park and in the community. She was punctual. She remained at the park until sundown. Most children had to be home 'before' the street lights flickered. At that time, the park officially closed. [When the lights flickered, the park was officially closed.]

Fast forward to the present. An internet search on Cann Park referred me to a My Space site advertising the park. A "gangsta" who called himself QA Four Life, bragged about the Cann Park "gangstas." His slogan for his "G's" on the park was, "If it ain't a thrill; it ain't real." Ironically, the word thrill had a significant meaning to the children in the park during the 1960s. Mrs. Sweeney sold thrills—frozen Kool-Aid in a Dixie cup with a Popsicle stick in the center—for 5¢. What a thrill!

From a social and economic stand point, the community is in a survival mode. The statistics tell the story.

Area   .0166 Square Miles
Population Density   6.567 People per Square Mile
Median Household Income $30,000
Median Age: Males   34.9
              Females   38.9
Single Mother Households   45%

Units with Mortgages   45%
Population Below Poverty Level   26.9%

      Organizations like the Community Planning and Development Services Department of Savannah, and the Cann-Jackson Park Neighborhood Association are making inroads into reviving the once thriving park and surrounding area. Through grants, home improvement and code correction funds, the area is on the road to a comeback. When I asked my parents if they had any intentions of selling their three homes in the area, their response was simple, "Someone who cares about the area must remain in the community."

Reflections on Cann Park
47th Street
Helen Zenobia Fletcher Scroggins

      "Mama may have, Papa may have, but God bless the child that has his own." This quote was used by my mother, Helen Brown Fletcher, during my youthful years. It's from the song, "God Bless The Child." It served as a motivation to me and my cousins.

      I am Helen Zenobia Fletcher Sroggins. The name Helen derived from my mother, Helen Brown Fletcher, and my maternal grandmother, Helen Robinson Brown. My middle name, Zenobia, derived from my paternal grandmother, Edna Zenobia Juhannes Fletcher. The name Zenobia can be traced back to a third century Syrian queen, who once ruled Egypt.

      My paternal grandmother's parents were from Bombay, India. They immigrated to Brunswick, Georgia. The family homes was located on Albany Street in Brunswick. They were merchants or store owners. My paternal grandparents were quite upset when my grandmother, Edna, married a West Indian who was from Jamaica. His name was Charles Fletcher. Edna and Charles eloped. Edna's father was so angry over the marriage that he chopped off his hand. Charles and Edna eventually moved to Savannah, Georgia. They resided at 519 East Perry Street. This area was known as the Old Fort.

29.

From the union of Charles and Edna Fletcher, my father, Edward Basel Fletcher, was born. He married my mother, Helen Brown. I was born April 15, 1948. I am an only child. We resided at 710 West 47th Street. This home was built in 1951, and was designed by my father. This street had a beautiful plot that ran down the center. This home holds great memories. Some of these memories are: the holidays, skating along the streets, fireworks, sparklers, lots of food in my mother's kitchen, and the pink and green walls representing my mother's membership in the Alpha Kappa Alpha Sorority ("Forever Green, Forever Clinging, Forever Climbing).

My paternal and maternal grandmothers lived with our family. However, my father's mother lived with us for nearly 20 years. She was a great seamstress. She would spend a great deal of time on her sewing machine. My maternal grandmother lived with us briefly, before going into a nursing home.

My greatest memory of grandparents centers on my great-grand-mother, Eva Dickerson Robinson. We called her 'Mama.' She died at the age of 98. She told me stories of growing up in Charleston, South Carolina. She was born in 1868, three years after the Civil War ended. Her father was a White man, who owned property on the Battery—Charleston's Waterfront. She told me these stories as I combed her hair at my grandmother's home, located at 927 West Victory Drive and 2704 Stevens Street.

In the early years of my growing up on 47th Street, it was unpaved, along with 48th Street. However, the greatness of 47th Street was found in the people who lived there. I want to pay homage to these neighbors by remembering them in this passage. Their names are as follows:

Rev. and Mrs. Benton	Mr. and Mrs. Burgess	Corine Davis
The Eadys	The Gibbs Family	Mrs. Irvin
Mr. and Mrs. Kelsy	Mr. and Mrs. Little	The Maynards (46th Street)
Mrs. McDuffy	Mr. and Mrs. Murvin	The Robinsons (46th Street)
Mrs. Russell	Roslyn Seamore	Harry Singleton
Essie Stewart	Mr. and Mrs. Stiles	Georgie Williams
Mr. and Mrs. Julius Williams		

I stand as a testament to the influence that one's family, home, environment, education, and religious training have in developing a whole person. The Brown, Juhannes, and Fletcher families instilled in me a sense of who I am. 710 West 47th Street gave me a sense of security. The neighbors and neighborhood gave me a sense of comfort. My educational training gave me a sense of the world around me. Finally, my Catholic religious training placed all of the above items into perspective.

Life On The Drive
Victory Drive
Christa Brown Stephens

In 1961 The Brown Family moved from Liberty City to 927 West Victory Drive. As children, moving to 'The Drive' meant we were rich. We were closer to our grandparents. Our father's mother, Mrs. Helen Robinson Brown, lived behind us in a garage apartment at 2704 Stevens Street. We called her Grandma Brown. North of Victory Drive, our mother's father, Deacon Edward Williams, Sr., lived two streets over from where we now live on Victory Drive. Papa, as we called him, lived at 1014 West 41st Street. To the south of us at 710 West 47th Street lived our father's sister, Mrs. Helen Brown Fletcher. We were surrounded by family and new found friends. Life in what is now called The Cann Park Community was full of excitement, along with clean and wholesome fun.

Grandma Brown was a thrifty lady who took pride in her property. She and Grandpa Chris paved a sidewalk from Victory Drive to Stevens Street Lane. Grandma Brown would sweep around the front of her door and sidewalk daily. She would even sweep Stevens. Street. At that time, the street was dirt, but it was swept clean as if it was a sidewalk. Immaculate was the word. Everything was spit-shined clean. My brothers would white-wash the fence and the barriers around the house. Grandman Brown would prepare dinner for some of the elderly neighbors in the community. One such person was Mrs. Mabel Marks. We would walk up the street to Mrs. Marks' home. Inside her home she had the most beautiful wood burning stove. We didn't stay long because it was very hot in her home. Then there was Mrs. Stewart who lived alone. We were always nervous about going to her house because she had many dogs. Once at Mrs. Stewart's home, you would hear the sounds of barking dogs from the back of the house racing to the front door. We would immediately put our feet at the screened door to keep the dogs from charging out of the door at us. Of course, work and chores always came before outside fun. **31.**

CANN PARK

Leisure Services Bureau
City of Savannah

For a long time Stevens Street was a dirt street. However, Victory Drive was a paved street where cars moved slowly up and down the street. Some of the families living on Victory Drive were:

The Barkleys	Rev. and Mrs. Blanton Black	Miss. Laura Densler
The Hamiltons	The Jefferson Family	Rev. and Mrs. Perry Jones
The Lamberts	The Lewis Family	Rev. and Mrs. Mims
The Orrs	The Pattersons	The Powells
Rev. and Mrs. Reeves	The Thomas Family	The Washingtons
The Williamses (Williams and Williams Funeral Home)		

It was normal for Black communities to have dirt streets. Nonetheless, we rode bicycles in mud holes, made mud pies, threw mud balls, played hide-n-seek, and shot marbles. We would venture down to Cann Park to play. There were merry-go-rounds. see-saws, swings, sliding boards, and fresh cool water from the water fountain. In addition, a thrilling game of kickball was always the hit of the day. However, if your street won, you'd better run home fast because a stick might be thrown at you for winning. It was all in fun.

Amaziah "Baby Brother" Smith, Edward Grant, Romey Anderson, Marion Smith, Matthew "Lil Mack" Brown, Leonard Brown, Christa Brown, Weasel, Sandra and Verdell Beasley would all join in for a game of Half-Rubber. The game called for a broom stick and a rubber ball cut in half. It took great skills to hit and pitch the ball.

On the whole, life was good. Yes, we were rich in love, family, friends and community.

VIII

LIBERTY CITY

Brick, Mortar and Rugged Hands
Liberty City

The name 'Liberty City' denotes a sense of freedom. During my formative years, Liberty City was a great place to discover, live, and come of age. In the mid to late 1950s, Liberty City's residential streets weren't paved. On our street, 55th, now called Lloyd Street, there were six families. They were the Browns, Bryants, Penningtons, Draytons, Browns (our cousins), and Greshams. There were no street lights. The roads were drained by ditches filled with tadpoles. However, there was one thing that was intangible—the freedom to be a child, in an environment in which we were encouraged to explore, run, discover and daydream.

Today, Liberty City is a thriving and stable community of African-American families with well kept homes. It is bordered by Staley Avenue, Mills B. Lane Boulevard, and William F. Lyons Parkway. Standing as the grand entrance to Liberty City, Dr. and Mrs. Henry Collier's mansion towered above the homes in the area. This home stood as a beacon—broadcasting the subliminal message that, "you can do it too." The Colliers were known for their grand houses. One can still be found on East Victory Drive and there was one once on East 37th Street.

Well established families had enduring roots in this community. Some of these families were:

The Johnsons	The Dingles	The Jones
The Palmers	The Paiges	The Bryants
The Matthews	The Smalls	The Bazemores
The Draytons	The Penningtons	The Barnes
The Greshams	The Smiths	The Browns
The Polites	The Colliers	The Moores
The Williams	The Beasleys	

These families are quite vivid in my memory. Many of the children in these families attended George W. DeRenne Elementary School, A. E. Beach Junior and Senior High Schools and even graduated from Savannah State College together.

There were four students who made their presence known in the schools in our area by volunteering their time. They were Mrs. Lottie Brown, Mrs. Lily Palmer, Mrs. Clara Bryant, and Mrs. Diane Page.

There were many others. However, I witnessed these mothers supervising their homes and their children with the assistance of their husbands. For many years Pastor Matthew Southall Brown, Sr., Pastor Emeritus of St. John Baptist Church, served as the president of the George W. DeRenne Elementary Parent Teacher Association (PTA). Because of his work in the school and the Liberty City Community, he was honored as Georgia's State Parent of the Year in 1960.

      Statistically, Liberty City still is a grounded community in Savannah. These figures validate this statement.

Area	1,681 Square Miles	
Population		2,962
Population Density	1.760 People per Square Mile	
Median Household Income		$37,285
Median Age:	Males 32.8	
	Females 36	

Average Household	2.8
Married Couples	44% (one of the highest in the Savannah area)
Single Mother Households	15%
Population Below Poverty Level	21.7%
Married Couple Families with Both Parents in the Home	42.1%

      I thank my parents for offering my siblings and me the Liberty to grow up in an environment in which we could be children, and have the sheltering love of a caring community.

A World of Color and Music
Liberty City
Maxine Brown Jones

My world was filled with color and music. I loved growing up in Savannah, Georgia; and I miss it dearly now.

As a child, I had the mindset that Liberty City was a city and it was for colored folks. I did not see whites or other races of people i Liberty City. Savannah seemed to be the colored-white melting pot.

Our little house on 55th Street in Liberty City was warm in the winter and hot in the summer. I remember running around the house—inside and out—playing. There was a living room, kitchen, bathroom, and two bedrooms. Daddy and Mother later added another bedroom, and a large den (It seemed large to me). The windows opened vertically and the little porch was hardly big enough for all of us to sit.

The streets were not paved and we had many friends to play with on those dirt streets. The Draytons lived at the end of our street. There were enough children in that family to make a basketball team. We played with them all of the time.

I would walk to Marcelite Dingle's house, Janice and Vernon Bryant's house, and Mrs. Johnson's house. We played with the Smith brothers (their sister was older). I remember going across the road to the Pennington's, but I do not remember playing with anyone.

Our little house seemed quite small when compared to Dr. Collier's house, which was at the entrance of the community. Although I took piano with his children, I never got to go inside their home or to play with them.

Our little house was filled with love. Daddy and mother were young parents raising four little children. I looked forward to Fridays. Mother would bring the best tasting orange juice home and we'd have fried fish, potato salad, brown'n serve rolls, and garden peas. Sometimes we had fish and grits. We ate in the living room on a table that was set up for dinner. After the 'backroom' was added, we had a place for the family to eat—a den area and a bedroom were added.

I had a doll house in the backyard built for me by my Godfather, Mr. Guilford. He and my Godmother lived on West Broad Street in what I called a 'huge' house. We echoed when we talked. I specifically remember the kitchen, living room and Mickey's (Carolyn Guilford) bedroom where we would play. Boarders who lived on another level made me uncomfortable.

Today, we have hardwood floors and plush carpeting. Our home had linoleum floors. Our little bathroom would fill with steam when I closed the door to take a bath. It seemed to take forever to get the steam off of the mirror so I could see myself. I often wonder how all six of us managed with one bathroom.

We watched school buses filled with White children pass us when school was in session, while we waited for parents to pick us up to take us to school. Our parents were car-pooling kids to school before it was a recognized asset. We went to schools in our community. George W. DeRenne Elementary was our community school and we loved it. There was hardly anyone that we did not know at the school. The sense of community was strong. I remember feeling loved by everyone.

Parents from Liberty City were strong PTA supporters and we would see various parents at school all of the time. Some of our teachers lived in Liberty City. We lived next door to Mr. Benny and Gwendolyn Brown, a musician and teacher. I always thought we were related to him. Mrs. Gresham lived on the corner. I loved to go to her house. She was a teacher and her home was absolutely lovely. She would talk to me about things in her home and I enjoyed listening.

The Bryants lived a street away and I would go play with Janice. Mrs. Bryant was always friendly and they too had a little house.

Daddy must have worked for a fuel oil company during those days because he smelled like fuel oil when he came home.

There was no central air or heat. In the winter, my sister and I would sleep together and daddy would put his big dark green army coat on top of the wool blanket to keep us warm. I don't know what they placed on my brothers. We were always warm.

Snakes seemed to have free reign, but that did not seem to bother us. 'Bushes' were on the side of our house and when we wanted to get even with a sibling, we simply threw something he/she liked into the 'bushes.' There was absolutely no retrieval because no one was brave enough to venture into the 'bushes.'

Mother was peaceful and quiet in that house. She would be in her bedroom talking to Mrs. James, Mrs. Bias or Mrs. Murvin on the telephone. I would sit in the hall listening.

Daddy and mother liked to entertain their friends. I remember the Biases and others coming out to our Liberty City home. I remember choco-late layer cakes every Sunday from Gottlieb……..

A Day of Protest
George W. DeRenne Elementary School
Ivy Paige Richardson

My sixth grade class at George W. DeRenne Elementary School went on strike. Our teacher was Mr. Smith. He lived on 44th Street close to Butler Presbyterian Church. His two story well kept home had the distinc-tion of being adjacent to the 'skating rink.' The 'rink' wasn't really for skating. It was a series of sidewalks used by children in the community.

Our strike began in the school's cafeteria. On the menu that day, fried chicken was featured. For dessert, a hot cinnamon roll was placed on our plates. As students, our portions of food were much smaller than our teachers'. On the day of the strike, we felt we deserved the same portion of food as our teachers.

Somehow the word reached our parents that we went on strike, refusing to do our class work. My mother couldn't drive and she didn't have a telephone. How she got the message that I was involved in a strike, to this day, I don't know. I believe one parent rounded up the others and they came to the school.

We were called to the cafeteria. We thought we had arrived. We had the cafeteria to ourselves. However, when we arrived, our PARENTS were there. My mother was sitting in my assigned seat! Boy did we cry that day! We didn't strike again.

The reflection showed me that our parents knew their neighbors from the first to the last street in Liberty City.

IX

DOWNTOWN SAVANNAH

When There Was A village
(Progress In The Midst Of Oppression)
Savannah

Hodding Carter, a Southern Progressive journalist and author, described Savannah in these terms, relative to Negro progress, "Savannah was the ideal place in the South for the Negro and his attainment. Savannah isn't a paradise, but it offers proof that separation and subjugation need not go hand in hand."

Savannah held a unique position in the lower South concerning Black property ownership. In the book, Black Property Owners in the South, 1790-1915, the author, Loren Schweninger documents Black property ownership particularly in Savannah, Georgia.

The Register of Free Persons of Color in Chatham County Georgia indicated that between 1817 and 1829 a total of 140 free persons of color had acquired some type of property. Ironically, since it was against the law in Savannah for freed Blacks to own real estate and slaves, they were forced to posses their real estate in the name of Whites and purchase buildings on someone else's land. The Georgia State Legislature passed a law in 1818 stating, "Blacks and Indians shall not be permitted to purchase or acquire any real estate or any slave or slaves, by direct conveyance, will, deed, contract, agreement or stipulation." If the law was violated, the property would be confiscated by the state and sold at public auction, with 10% of the proceeds going to the informant. One year later, the law was repealed except for the cities of August, Darien and Savannah—cities with substantial Black populations.

According to Father Charles L. Hoskins' book, Out of Yamacraw and Beyond: Discovering Black Savannah, African Americans flocked to Savannah immediately after the Civil War, settling on the fringes of the city. He further states that many homes were built for Blacks in the northern section of what was called Brownville or Brownsville. The earliest houses, known as Meldrim Row, were built on West 33rd (Victory Drive) and 34th Streets.

Loren Schweninger's book, Black Property Owners in the South, 1790-1915, documents specific names of property owners in Savannah. Examples of these persons are as follows:

- Polly Baptiste owned a building on lot #5 in the Green Ward.
- Benjamin Reizne owned a building on ¼ of a lot in Yamacraw.
- Leah Beard owned a small house on the lot of M. H. McAllister, a White resident.

Dr. Schweninger offers a "Biographical Listing of Prosperous Blacks in the South Between 1870-1915." Savannah residents have been highlighted below:

- Property valued in excess of $500.00

Anthony Odingsells   Susan Jackson
Louis Murault   Hannah Leon
John Gibbons Andrew Marshall
Polly Spein
- Property valued between $20,000 - $49, 9999

Daniel ButtonJohn H. Deveaux
William RoyalD. C. Scruggs
- Property valued between $50,000 - $99,999

G. A. Bowen

- Property valued in excess of $100,000
Anthony K. DesVerney (once known as the wealthiest Black man in Savannah)

Probate Court Records of Chatham County Georgia, dating back to 1852 verify the ownership of property by Rev. Andrew Marshall, pastor of First African Baptist Church. In his will, his property bequeathed to his family included land and a building at the corner of Fahm and Bryan Streets and in the Village of Gall. He was also a shareholder in the Marine and Fire Insurance Bank of Georgia.

The following years document Black participation in real estate in Savannah, Georgia:

1823   Sixty-four Blacks owned their own homes in Savannah.
1826   Among 184 adult men and women in Chatham Country, 67 owned property or approximately one out of three.

1837   The economic turn down (Panic of 1837) caused some Blacks to lose their homes.

1852   According to the Chatham County Savannah Tax Assessment List, Blacks controlled real estate appraised at $18,500.00 and personal property appraised at $20,015.00.

Finally, in Abbey Lincoln's September 1966 article entitled, Who will Revere the Black Woman?, she writes, "Mark Twain said, in effect, that when a country enslaves a people, the first necessary job is to make the world feel that the people to be enslaved are sub-human. The next job is to make his fellow-countrymen believe that the man is inferior and then, the unkindest cut of all is to make that man believe himself inferior." The general white community has told us in a million different ways and in no uncertain terms that God and nature made a mistake when it came to fashioning us and ours." I say, Thank God the aforementioned property owners didn't buy into this myth. They used their so called inferior status to improve their economic stature.

Reflections: Downtown Savannah
Leonard Brown

It was easy to travel the safe streets of my neighborhoods. Abduction of a child was foreign in my commUNITY.

In the 1960s, life for me was a pleasant experience. Even though this country was in turmoil (assassinations, wars, student protests, Civil Rights Movement), my sheltered life centered on the west side of Savannah, Georgia. My mode of transportation was a silver and maroon bicycle, a Schwinn I believe. It took me through and to a world of visual history. My most pleasant rides came on Thursdays. This was the day I rode from my parents' home on Victory Drive to the home of Duchess Judy von Allen, as she called herself my music teacher. Duchess von Allen was an older white lady that lived on East Harris Street, in an old set of 18th century row houses just off Lafayette Square, in the Historic District. She was quite eccentric. Her music studio was very dark, with only one light glowing over her upright piano. The heavy dark floor-to-ceiling drapes blocked the calming rays of the sun. My focus had to only be on the musical notes found on the sheet music.

After my music lesson ended, the highlight of my day began. I had the opportunity to ride my bicycle leisurely home. The routes were unpredictable: Bull Street, Forsyth Park, Henry Street, West Broad Street, West Victory Drive…. On my most daring days, I would travel down West Broad Street to 45th Street to enjoy the ease of the 'Infamous 45th Street Hill.' On this street sat some of the most beautiful and well-kept homes, in my estimation.

As I made my way home, I enjoyed the comfort and safety of my segregated community. These sites were noticeable features of my rides home:

1. The Kiah Museum/Home
2. Charity Hospital
3. Cann Park
4. Doctor's Row
5. St. Matthews Episcopal Church
6. The Star Theater
7. Bynes-Royal Funeral Home
8. The beautiful tree lined 37th Street
9. The Pickens' home swimming pool
10. The evenly placed palm trees and azalea plants on West Victory Drive
11. Butler Presbyterian Church
12. The 'skating rink'(a series of sidewalks on West Victory Drive)
13. Florance Street School
14. Jackson's Convenience Store
15. Al's Cleaners
16. Beaver's Barbershop
17. The Seventh Day Adventist Church
18. Home (West Victory Drive)

A roll call can be done of the families and persons living on certain streets. These families and persons created a sense of stability for a child, such as myself growing up in the area. Adult eyes peered from the homes, reporting any misbehavior of children living—and those not living—in the area. These adults did something foreign by today's standards—they communicated from their porches, driveways, and backyards with their neighbors.

Let's call the roll of some of the streets containing individuals and families who anchored the Cuyler-Brownville (Brownsville) and Cann Park Communities, as I recall.

36th   Kiah, Futch, Dash, Jamieson, Cosby, Jackson, Gilbert, Fonvielle, Belcher

37th   Guilford, Bland, Eberhardt, Hill, Bryant, McAfee

38th   Green, Fleming, McDew

39th   Williams, Thornton, Bryant, Law, Fields, Ford, Allen, Rickenbacker

40th   Harden, Hall

41st   Williams, Blalock, Kelson, Harden, Walker, Cobbins, Crawford, McMillan, Pickney, Gartrell, Shanks, Cargo

42nd   Scott, Stripling, Beckett, Haven, Deveaux, Raines, Mathias, Stringer, Manigo, Lovett, Robinson, Thompson

44th   Moore, May, Hopkins, Andrews, Flood, Leak, Simmons, Williams, Crawford, Stewart, Caution, Burns, Benward, Smith, Densler, Jackson

45th   Sexton, Cargo, Freeman, Delaware, Gibbs, Sessions, James, McDew, Wilson, Blake, Bolden, Williams, Hicks, Anthony, Stevens, Bedgood, DeLong, Strickland

46th   Maynard, Guilford

47th   Fletcher, Benson, Williams, Irvin, Murvin, Eady, Scarborough

48th   Black, Stewart, Uncle John and Emily
        (I never knew their surnames)

Victory Drive
        Brown, Jefferson, Ladson, Harrington, Marks, Orr, Thomas, Hamilton, Lambert, Washington, Densler, Lewis, Daniels, Black, Wright, Law, Jones, Powell, Rainey, Mims, Boston, Holmes, Patterson, Grace, Jones, Bland, Hall

Hopkins Street Johnson, Smith, Kennedy, Law, Dean, Wade

This list by no means represents the un-named families who resided on these corridors. It does represent the families and individuals my family directly and indirectly knew. These families and individuals represented the best in Savannah's African-American community in terms of education, spirituality, hard work, values, homeownership, stability, community involvement, and leadership. Unknowingly, they showed me and many other children in the community what it was like to raise a family, and to own and maintain a home.

African Americans living in the Cuyler-Brownville (Brownsville) Community, Cann Park Community, Liberty Park, Thunderbolt, Derrick's Inn, Hilton Head Island and Savannah's Downtown District weren't by any means rich. They were however, wealthy in ways one couldn't put a price on, during my youth.

- It was the type of wealth I don't feel in my present COMMUNITY.
- The wealth of a warm and hardy greeting
- The wealth of mature trees
- The wealth of an over the fence conversation with my neighbors
- The wealth of children at play
- The wealth of enjoying a quiet evening on my front porch
- The wealth of friends visiting friends
- The wealth of seeing families going to church on Sundays

Anita Singleton Prather, a native of Beaufort, South Carolina, writes in her description of her youth on the sea islands of Beaufort County, South Carolina, "I couldn't see through young eyes, the treasures of wealth I had growing up here in the late 1950s."

LaPageville
Dorothy Shavers Brown

LaPageville was a small community of African Americans who worked for the Seaboard Railroad Company. Once a neighborhood of pride and dignity, it soon became a forgotten place of despair and pain. It was a place for a lot of firsts for my family. My grandfather (Mingo Shavers) was the first Black man in the community to hold the position of foreman for the Seaboard Railroad Company. The Shavers family was the first to own a car in the community. My mother and my aunt attended Catholic school.

My fondest memory would be before I started school. We ran through grassy fields picking plums from our plum orchard. Rolling down the green dunes on the golf course and trying not to be caught by the White attendant gave us a great thrill. At five years old I skipped to the bus stop, waiting for my siblings to arrive from school to hear their stories and adventures. Most of my early years were years of fun and excitement; such as picking blackberries in the Summer and in the Fall trying to be the one who could find the largest pecans.

These fond memories soon turned to years of pain and heartache. Tragedy would come to find the Shavers Family. After the death of my grandfather, life changed for my family. When I started school I was told that I couldn't participate in the May Day celebration because my mother couldn't afford to purchase the dress. I realized that where I lived brought on a sense of disdain from other people who didn't live in our community. I learned early that LaPageville wasn't a place you told people you resided. My worse memory was walking late at night with my older sisters to pick up my mother who was a maid for a White family. As we walked home, a car approached us with young White boys in the car. One of them got out of the car and stabbed my mother in the back. It was only by the grace of God that she had on a layered coat. The blade didn't penetrate her back, it only nicked her back. We had to hide under a house and wait because the car returned looking for us. We stayed there until the break of dawn. It was at this point I began to hate the name LaPageville and what it represented. It would be years before I would even tell my friends where I lived for fear of them looking down on me.

Our God said, "Your ending would be greater than my beginning."

Because of where I started, I can proudly say I lived in the LaPageville Community. Thus from humble beginnings God would shape and mold me into the person I am today.

Reflections: Pastor Matthew Southall Brown, Sr.
The 1920s on Hartridge Street

Growing up on Hartridge Street in Savannah, Georgia was a wonderful experience. Located between two main thoroughfares, Price and East Broad Streets, a unique and diverse community was found. The street was unpaved from Price to Bowen Streets. At the edge of the Hartridge Street cobble stones were found. Cars traveling along Hartridge Street created what we called ruts or grooves. When it rained we would use these ruts to float our homemade boats.

A store stood at the corner of Price and Hartridge Streets. It was called Dooley-Harry. The owners were of Irish origin. The store was stocked with the basic necessities for a typical family. Black families who shopped here could establish credit, as a means of paying for their goods. My father, Christopher F. Brown, who was a postal employee, had an account at this store.

My parents owned a duplex on Hartridge Street. The addresses were 519 and 521. Our family, the Browns (Christopher F. Brown, Sr., Helen Robinson Brown, Christopher F. Brown, Jr., Eva Brown DeVault, Helen Brown Fletcher, and Matthew Southall Brown, Sr.), lived at 519. The Felder Family lived at 521. The layout of the home was simple yet comfortable. It consisted of a living room, a small dining room, two bedrooms, a bathroom, and a kitchen. The house had a large backroom that was used for sleeping, eating, and playing. There was a large backyard. In this backyard my father built an out- house, not to be confused with an outdoor toilet. This was a guest house used for visiting relatives from Columbia, South Carolina, my mother's home. Beyond the backyard was what I called "the green." It consisted of about four vacant lots. This space was used by the children of the neighborhood for playing on the lush green grass.

The Felder Family, that lived next door, had a son named John Junior. We were playmates and often found ourselves at the

Dooley-Harry Store. It seemed as though John always had a few more coins in his pocket than I. Consequently, I would spend his money on lots of candy...Mary Janes, BB Bats and Cow Tails.

Towering over the residential structures was St. John Baptist Church. In 1885 the church was constituted. It was built in 1891; under the leadership of Father William Gray and a band of believers. During my youth, Dr. Evans Oliver Sylvester Cleveland served as pastor of the church. Under Dr. Cleveland's leadership, the renowned 80 Voice Chorus was created and the magnificent Moeller Pipe Organ was purchased. Ironically, in 1969 I was called to pastor this Church. I served as its pastor for 35 years. In another twist, the graduating class of Cuyler-Beach High School held its commencement at St. John Baptist in 1946. My wife, Lottie Williams (Brown) was in this class. "The Lord moves in Mysterious Ways." Finally, I remember a large sycamore tree standing on the northwest side of the church. This tree served as the church's property line.

Our community had an interesting combination of neighbors. As I previously stated, Hartridge Street was a diverse and unique place to live. Some of the neighbors I remember were:

Lucy Williams Lucas - She as a business woman whose profession was that of a seamstress. I remember her house having a 'crow's nest.' Metaphorically, a crow's nest is the highest point of a structure. The crow's nest of her home consisted of a series of windows from the ground floor to the second story.

Sis. Boyd – As I remember, Sis. Boyd lived alone. She often wore an apron. She took an interest in me and I often sat in her lap as a child. I remember going to visit her one day and found her deceased on the floor. The room was filled with flies. To this day I despise flies.

Clarence Perkins, Sr. – He had a reputation of being a well read and intelligent man. He worked for several attorneys in downtown Savannah. Because of the knowledge gained from his profession, many people sought advice from him.

Mr. and Mrs. Channey – They owned their duplex. They lived on the corner of Hartridge and Bowen Streets. Surrounding their yard was a tin fence. Fences during these days were built to keep children inside the yard, not to keep people out.

Dr. Edward Verner, MD - He lived on Hartridge Street but attended St. Phillip AME Church on West Broad Street. His son, Edward Jr., became close friends with my brother, Christopher, Jr.

Rev. Ross – He served as the pastor of Second Baptist Church, now referred to as Second African Baptist Church. The church's parsonage was found on Hartridge Street, which housed Rev. Ross and his family. In later years, Rev. Perry and his family lived in the parsonage.

James R. Middleton – A carpenter by trade, Mr. Middleton resided at 521 Hartridge Street, the former home of the John Felder Family.

On Hartridge Street and neighboring streets, my family had friends who served as role-models and mentors. Some of these families were as follows:

Mr. and Mrs. Callen – They lived on Huntington Street. Mr. Callen was an insurance man by profession; and lived quite well. He was a relative of Frank Callen.

Captain John Starr – A resident of Gaston Street, he served as a licensed boat pilot of the steam vessel, Yamacraw. He was a well respected and learned man. Captain Starr was trained in the United States Coast Guard.

The Chambers Family – This family lived on Huntington Street. Their son Eddie was a close friend of mine. It is believed that this family was Black Puerto Ricans.

Hall Street was considered a bad street. I was forbidden to play or be seen on this street. People who were considered as alcoholics frequented this street.

Finally, at the corner of Hartridge and East Broad Streets, stood East Broad Street School. I attended this school and St. Benedict Catholic School just around the corner on Gaston and East Broad Streets. When my family moved to the west side to occupy the new home my father had purchased (925 West Victory Drive), I attended Florance Street School. Today, East Broad Street School is a senior citizens facility. It is called St. John's Villa. This conversion took place during my pastorate of St. John Baptist Church.

"The Lord Moves in Mysterious Ways."

Eddie Lamar Jones, Jr.
Millen Street
West Savannah

I am Eddie Lamar Jones, Jr., the son of Mayola Hills Jones and Eddie Lamar Jones, Sr. I was born in Savannah, Georgia on November 22, 1948. My place of birth was Charity Hospital located on West 36th Street. The segregated facility was organized by Doctors Cornelius and Alice McKane in 1853.

My family's roots can be traced to a home in West Savannah. This home was located at 234 Millen Street. It was owned by my great-grandmother, Peggy Hills. She purchased this home in 1929. Two renovations and additions were done to this home in 1934 and 1958. Ms. Polly Hills, my grandmother and Mayola Hills Jones, my mother, resided in this home for many years. This home is still occupied by members of my family.

Young people who lived in the area attended Tompkins Elementary and Tompkins High Schools. One of my favorite high school teachers was Mr. Charles Brannen. He was an instructor in the Social Science Department. He was my history teacher in 1965. Ironically, Mr. Brannen was a member of the church my father-in-law pastored, St. John Baptist Church. His family, the Wileys, were foundational members of this church.

Upon graduation from Tompkins High School in 1967, I entered Savannah State College. A year later I was in Vietnam. I served in this conflict for one year and a half, in the area of intelligence gathering. During this era the draft was in place, the Selective Service. However, I volunteered my service to my country serving in the United States Marine Corp.

In 1971, I returned to Savannah and Savannah State College.

This year was and is significant to me because I married Maxine Brown. We were married at St. John Baptist Church at 2:30 p.m. Rev. Matthew Southall Brown, Sr., Maxine's father, and Rev. Edward Lamar Ellis, Jr., Maxine's uncle, performed the ceremony.

Our union in marriage has lasted 46 years. Eddie Lamar Jones, III and Katea Jheree Jones Watson are our off springs. Our children have produced five grandchildren. They are Khalil, Alphonso, Nyla, Nia, and Derico. Nicole Samuels Jones and Derico Watson are our daughter and son-in-law.

Career wise, I hold the distinction of being the first African American to be employed by the U.S. Postal Service as a Manager of Distribution Operations Service.

My life has been filled with adventures and traveling. I have engaged myself in many projects throughout my life. Some of these are biking, photography, leatherwork, house design, landscaping, graphic design, and travel. Our home at 6 Davidson Avenue in Savannah, Georgia, was a home design project of mine.

To expose my family to challenging experiences, I exposed them to traveling. On many trips we were the only African Americans. We traveled from the East Coast to the West Coast. Our son, at a young age, traveled to Hawaii, Australia, and New Zealand. He traveled with the National Chorus. We continue to take family centered trips.

Finally, my guiding philosophy in life has centered on these two statements: 1 "Give 100%, whether someone is watching you or not." 2. "Complete a task given to you.

From Monroe to Savannah
First Bryan Baptist Church
Rev. Edward Ellis, Jr.

I am Edward Lamar Ellis, Jr. I was born in Monroe, Georgia, Walton County, in the year 1932. My parents were Edward Ellis, Sr., and Phenolia Robertson Ellis. My father's profession was that of a barber. My mother was a homemaker. My siblings are Gloria, Bobby and Alvin (deceased).

As a young man I attended Carver High School in Monroe, Georgia. I also attended Fort Vally State College. I consider my years at Fort Valley the most rewarding. I say this because I was greatly influenced by Dean Walter McCall. I served as his assistant. This position afforded me the opportunity to meet and dialogue with a young Dr. Martin Luther King, Jr. Dr. King was invited to speak for Religious Emphasis Week at Fort Valley College in 1955. This event was not widely attended by the student body. However, Dr. King delivered a sermon entitled, "Three Dimensions of a Complete Life." This sermon was delivered on a Thursday night. The next night there was standing room only. This speech made a lasting impression on me. In conversing with Dr. King, I received a new perspective on entering into the ministry.

Fort Valley College inspired me academically, socially and religiously. I was the recipient of the Best All Around Student Award and the Henry A. Hurst Prize in 1956; and I served as the student body president. Having served in the military for three years seven months and 21 days prior to attending college, gave me a greater appreciation of my college experience.

Upon my graduation from Fort Valley, I returned to Monroe, Georgia. God had a plan. A young Spelman woman, Lillian Sharon Williams, had been employed in the school system in Monroe, Georgia, as a music teacher. We were assigned to the same school. I met my future with in 1960.

I married Lillian Sharon Williams in 1962. In 2012, we celebrated 50 years of marriage. From our union three children were born—Sharon, Joia, and Edward III. All of our children are college educated. Edward III followed the calling of the Lord into the ministry. We have six grandchildren.

Throughout my life I have engaged in several occupational fields. These occupations were teaching, corrections, and social work. My greatest calling came when I accepted the call to preach the Gospel. This calling led me, ironically, to Savannah, Georgia, the home of my wife. In 1951 I was called to pastor First Bryan Baptist Church. This congregation was organized in 1788. The community in which the church is found, Yamacraw Village, is where my wife was raised. Her family was the third one to move into this housing facility. The family resided behind the church.

While at First Bryan, there were four major accomplishments I feel that impacted the neighborhood and local community. They were:

1.   The celebration of the church's bicentennial in 1988;
2.   The church underwent massive renovations—restoring the gothic sanctuary, stained glass windows were installed during this period;
3.   The relationship between the neighborhood and the church was our greatest accomplishment. As a congregation, we invited and introduced the citizens of Yamacraw Village to First Bryan through our outreach ministries;
4.   Dr. Charles Elmore completed a comprehensive history of the church in 2002.

After 25 years of service to First Bryan, I retired from the day-to-day pastorate of the church. I was asked to stay on for another year, until another minister was called. However, I haven't retired from the service of the Lord.

Two hundred and thirty-one miles (231 miles) changed my life forever. This is the distance between Monroe, Georgia and Savannah, Georgia.

X

THUNDERBOLT

"Where Savannah Meets the Sea"
Thunderbolt

As a young child, I remember a song being sung about this town—"Thunderbolt, Thunderbolt, Thunderbolt was an Indian town. When the lightning struck the ground, the Indians came all around. Thunderbolt was an Indian town."

Legend has it that the town of Thunderbolt began when a bolt of lightning struck the ground and a freshwater spring appeared on Wilmington Bluff, Native Americans were the first inhabitants. In 1856, the town of Thunderbolt was incorporated as Warsaw; beginning its history as a processing port for the fishing community.

Prominently located in Thunderbolt, Georgia, The Industrial College for Colored Youth, now know as Savannah State University, stands. In 1890 it was established by the Georgia General Assembly and the federal government's Merrill Act, for the education of colored youth. The initial sessions or classes were held at Baxter Street School on Athens, Georgia during the months of June to August in 1891. In October of the same year, it was moved to the present site. Granting its first degree in 1898, it is the first public academic institution of higher learning started for African Americans in Georgia. The school's first president was Richard R. Wright.

Joseph Derrick, a grand uncle of mine, was on the faculty; teaching in the Agriculture Department. In June 1973, I received a Bachelor of Science Degree in the areas of Education and the Social Sciences from this institution. It was at this location that I saw educated African-American men and women of distinction—Dean Walton, Kiah, Boston, Oliver, Payne, Elmore, Yancey, Johnson (Mayor), Milton, Gadsden, Thorpe, Woodhouse, Mobley, Waddell, Campbell, Jackson, Black, Freeman, Clemmons, Robinson, Owens, Braithwaite, Lumpkin, Waters, Harmon, Byers, Stokes, Blalock and the staff members who carried themselves in a very professional manner. The Brown Family legacy is still present at Savannah State University. Kiesha Brown is a math instructor. She represents the fourth generation.

Looking at some data about Thunderbolt, it remains a stable community for African Americans.

Area   1.3 Square Miles
Population   2,649
Population Density   2,079 People per Square Mile
Median House Value $91,000
Median Age: 41.9
African-American Population   32.4%
Distance from City of Savannah   3.3 Miles

The words of the first President of Savannah State University, Richard R. Wright, when asked how the college was progressing, can be used to describe the plight of the African-American population in Thunderbolt, "Just tell them we are rising."
Memories of Thunderbolt and Its People
Marian E. Butler Marshall

I was born in Savannah but live in this town called Thunderbolt. Thunderbolt was really nice back in the day. I can remember the fishing boats and the fishermen that were always on the bluff. There were many stores and fish markets on the bluff. I remember that the chief of police was a very large man by the name of Chief Leonard. He smoked a very large cigar. He would come to our school (Powell Laboratory Elementary School) which was on the Savannah State College Campus. Chief Leonard would talk to the students about safety and community activities. I remember him giving out fruit and candy at Christmas time. We would meet on the campus at the band stand and sing Christmas carols as a community activity; this was the entire community—Blacks and Whites—the entire community! Powell Laboratory School was a part of Savannah State College and Chatham County Schools. When I was in the fifth grade, it was taken over by the county and was moved to a new location. We had a new school. About this time I entered sixth grade. The school was completely built. The name of the school became Sol. C. Johnson. I always tell people I had the privilege of walking to elementary, middle, high school and college.

I remember my street being a dirt road and we lived at a dead end. They tell me Savannah had trolley cars before I was born. They turned around right in front of my house. I don't remember trolley cars but I remember the dirt road and the dead end. In order to go to my church, which was down the street, we had to go through the woods on a path.

Now, of course, all the paths are streets and roads. All of our neighbors were people who were born in that neighborhood or they were professors and their families that moved into the neighborhood over the years. We all knew each other and looked out for each other and each other's things. My Aunt Clara was a watchman, because she would sit on her porch and watch to see what was going on. She would do this until the day that she passed. Older women in the neighborhood would teach the young girls and boys how to conduct themselves and they didn't mind scolding you and telling your parents why they did it. Therefore, you had double punishment. The Sweet Field of Eden Society, Sunday School and Baptist Training Union (BTU) were groups that taught young people. We also had Girl and Boy Scout Troops. When they say it takes a village to raise a child, I experienced this first-hand. The people in my neighborhood knew the children and looked out for us. My parents would want to know who that child is, and who are their people? They would seek them out or we would not find ourselves playing with them.

My most pleasant memory is of my family sitting outside on the porch, under the large oak tree in my front yard, during the spring and summer times. We would listen to the stories our parents told of their childhood and relatives. The lightening bugs would be flying and the frogs and crickets could be heard. That was the high point of the day. My most disturbing memory was a very terrible thing. Mr. B. J. James, who owned the corner store near the campus, was stabbed. This was the first murder in Thunderbolt that I recalled. We were all upset. The worst part was that it was someone that lived in the community. It was found out that the young man was on drugs, something that was not as common as it is today.

XI

DERRICK'S INN

"A Placid Cocoon"
Derrick's Inn

Highway 17 South or Ogeechee Road takes you back in time to a road that leads you to a family of determination—the Derricks: Joseph and Mamie. The year was c. 1929 when the Derricks purchased 23 acres of land on a marsh to raise a family and farm. Derrick's Inn Road, a neatly graded dirt road carried many members of my family to this destination. The Burns, Stewarts, Browns, Fletchers, Camerons, Webbs, Williams, Herrings, Millers, Robinsons, Jones, Poythress, Stephens, Whitleys, Scroggins, Whites, and many of the old Savannah families.

Entering the property you find large majestic trees that have been on this compound since my youth. Guarding the property's entrance, these trees guide you to the family home which still stands. It was in this house, seated in the dining room, that I was introduced to my father's family—the Burns and Browns. It was in this home that I learned about the Browns and Burns cemetery plot in Laurel Grove South. It was on this land that an appreciation was gained for the care and concern of nature, before the Green Movement became popular. It was at this place that I understood the meaning of hard work, resilience and resourceful- ness.

Geese, pigs, cows, mules, chickens, ponies, dogs and ducks were regular inhabitants on this land. Aside from the animals, visitors from all over the African-American community of Savannah and the South would visit the Derricks. Tranquility was the order of the day. A walk to the plowed fields with Uncle Joe Derrick would reveal the dream for the land—a half-moon hotel. Visitors would very seldom leave Derrick's Inn empty handed—eggs, pears, pecans, vegetables, sugarcane, buttermilk, and clabber (the forerunner to yogurt) were mainstays.

A few yards from the family's home was a salt water creek. There was a rickety old wharf used for fishing, diving and dating. When the tide was low, just below your knees, crabbing was done. A rock on a string with rotten chicken meat would yield bushels of blue crabs. Casting with a circular net would get you shrimp and fish. Laura Derrick West, our cousin, was the expert at casting. Aunt Laura, as we called her (we were taught as children never to call adults by their first name), was Uncle Joe's right hand. She could repair just about anything on the farm, and at

George W. DeRenne Elementary School where she taught.

Derrick's Inn brought a temporary 'end' to many African-American stress filled lives in the segregated South. It served as a haven, a retreat, and a place to restore one's sense of self—"A Placid Cocoon." Living at Derrick's Inn

Laura Derrick Webb

I am Laura Derrick Webb. My parents were Rev. Joseph and Mamie Brown Derrick. I spent my formative years at two homes. One home was at 617 Park Avenue and the other home was located at 422 Derrick's Inn Road in Savannah, Georgia. I was born on the campus of Georgia State College on December 13, 1923, where my father taught agriculture.

In January of 1943, I took advantage of a training program offered by the United States government in Jesup, Georgia. So many of the young men were drafted into the service to fight in World War II that young women were being trained to work in various activities such as building airplanes, and paper work. My first assignment was in Los Angeles, California. Later I was transferred to Sacramento, California to repair radios. While in Sacramento, I enrolled in Sacramento Junior College to take classes in secretarial subjects. My next assignment was in San Bernadina, California to repair airplane engines and to make engine parts. My last assignment was in the tool shop. When I returned to my shift one day, the supervisor told me that the general wanted to see me. The general asked if I would like to be transferred to Washington, D.C. to work in the Office of War Information. I said yes, because it meant that I would be closer to Savannah. First, I was assigned to work in Arlington, Virginia then to Washington, D.C. While in Washington, I attended Howard University, taking courses in math and science. At the end of World War II in 1945, I returned to Savannah and enrolled in South Carolina State College; majoring in science. My Bachelor and Masters degrees were earned from this college. I also hold a Professional Diploma from Atlanta University. In 1972 I received a Specialist in Administration.

My work experience began in Hogansville, Georgia in 1950 teaching high school science. In 1953 I returned to Savannah and was employed to teach at DeRenne Elementary School until 1963. After desegregation, I was assigned to Bloomingdale, then Gould Elementary. I retired in June 1986.

Living at Derrick's Inn there were friends, acquaintances and family that came from the city, and as far as….the West, East, North and South to spend from two to three weeks on what was once an old plantation. The land was purchased while daddy was still a student at Georgia State College (Savannah State University). There were always fresh vegetables from the farm and seafood from the river. Holidays, such as Memorial Day, Independence Day, and Labor Day, brought many people for fun and games (boating, swimming, crabbing, merry-go-round, and baseball) and lots of other activities.

I lived at 617 West Park Avenue with my Aunts: Duchy-Laura Brown Baker Stewart, Jennie Brown, Rosa Brown, and Mary E. F. Burns. While growing up they did not want my sisters and me to attend a one-room country school. While living at 617, I attended Florance Street Elementary, Cuyler Junior High, and Alfred E. Beach High Schools. Oft times I would live at Derrick's Inn and ride the bus to school. Because I loved the outdoors, I lived mostly at home with my mother and father, where I played with my animals.

Our family, the Browns and Burns, were members of First African Baptist Church. Our family moved their membership to Beth Eden Baptist Church in the early twenties. At the age of twelve, I was baptized by Rev. Clark. Becoming a Christian became the focal point of my life. As a young adult, I taught Sunday School and later served for twelve years as Superintendent of the Sunday School. My membership was moved to First African Baptist Church about ten years ago.

617 West Park Avenue and Derrick's Inn
Sarah Derrick Herring

I was born at 617 West Park Avenue on March 1, 1929. I was born in the home my grandaunt had built from her teacher's salary in the early 1900s. Miss. Mary E. F. Burns purchased the land, built a house, and a store on Park Avenue Lane. When she saved enough money, she had the two story apartment built at 617 West Park Avenue. The downstairs apartment was for her and her mother, Lydia Burns. The upstairs apartment was for her sisters—Janie Burns Brown and her children. The home had indoor plumbing and electricity. The other homes on the street had out-door plumbing.

Four generations lived at 617 at one time or another. The home served as an anchor for the family. Various relatives and friends visited often. Some of them were colorful and enjoyable, such as Christopher F. Brown, Sr. and Jr. Christopher, Jr. always visited after he attended a funeral, demonstrating the actions of the mourners. He would put on a real show! He was always dressed professionally. I was always happy for a visit from Chris. He treated me like a little sister. Christopher Sr. was another character. He was jovial. He loved to pinch my cheeks. Having him to come visit was a pleasure.

Before the oil heaters were used to heat the home, fireplaces were used for heat. I loved when winter came because the elders would sit and tell stories about their childhood. They said that grandma (Lydia Burns) would awaken them early on Monday morning to whip them, if they miss behaved on Sunday. No work was done on Sunday—only church, dinner, and visiting friends. The other thing that was enjoyable at 617 was sitting in front of the floor model radio and listening to the various programs. Looking back, this was really funny.

Having dinner with the family was important. This is missing from so many families now. We ate together—the young and the old. We enjoyed pleasant discussions. The children were heard as well as the adults.

Whenever Aunt Sarah Burns Orr White and her husband, Rev. White, were visiting, we had evening services. Dada (Sarah) would play hymns and Rev. White would read Scriptures from the Bible and say an Evening Prayer⊠If I have wounded any soul today. Rev. White was a missionary minister. He went all over the United States; raising money for the C.M.E. Churches.

Derrick's Inn was my other home. My father, Rev. Joseph W. Derrick, began purchasing property in 1915, while attending Georgia State Industrial College for Colored Youth now Savannah State University. After graduating, he taught agriculture and ran the Boarding Department. He and my mother, Mamie A. Brown Derrick, moved from the college in 1929.

Both of my parents possessed good work ethics and were determined that their children would also. Everyone was assigned a task. You were to complete your task perfectly, or near perfectly, in a timely manner. We worked hard, but there was also time provided for fun.

Indoors we played cards, American and Chinese checkers. Outdoors we played ring plays under the moonlight. Daddy would make a smoke to keep the bugs from eating us alive. Crabbing was one of my favorite things to do. After catching the crabs, daddy would make a big fire under the iron wash tub, when the water got boiling hot, the crabs were put in the tub. The other thing that was enjoyable was dancing on the pavilion. After the picnic people left, the relatives would take to the floor. My mother and my aunt, Helen Robinson Brown the mother of Pastor Matthew S. Brown, Sr., would call themselves doing the Joe Louis. They would roll up their fists and see which one could out dance the other one. Everyone got a kick out of this. Just writing about it makes me smile.

Living up to my parents' expectations of hard work and education, I received degrees in the areas of Business Administration, and Education. These degrees were obtained from SSU and AAU. I did further studies at Old Dominion University, Norfolk State and Atlanta University. These educational experiences afforded me opportunities to work in the following capacities: Records Secretary (SSU); Troup, Chatham, Efffingham Counties Boards of Education; YWCA Center Program Director (Savannah), Executive Director Phyllis Wheatly Branch YWCA (Norfolk, Virginia).

Professionally I hold membership in several organizations. They are as follows: National Council of Negro Women, Georgia Association of Retired Educators, Georgia Association of Garden Clubs, American Business Women's Association (Victory Chapter), Variety Garden Club, and the Majestic Social Club.

At the age of nine I was baptized in Beth Eden Baptist Church. I was a member of this church for over 50 years. Presently, I am a member of First African Baptist Church—the church of the Brown-Burns families.

He Walked Him Back to Christ
617 West Park Avenue and Derrick's Inn Road
Albert Benjamin Cameron, Jr.

I am Albert Benjamin Cameron, Jr. My parents were Mollie Derrick Cameron and Albert "A. B." Benjamin Cameron, Sr. I have one sister, Laura Michelle Cameron Woods, and a deceased brother, Ronald Cameron (March 2, 2012). I am the father of three children: two daughters, Mia and Rita; and one son, Albert III. Additionally, I have six grandchildren. I am married to Pamela Lavon Cameron.

Joseph Derrick and Mamie Brown Derrick, my grandparents, had a great influence on my life. I moved to their 100 acre farm at the age of six months. I remained in their care until I reached my high school years (15). My grandparents' entrepreneurial spirits were lessons that have lasted me a lifetime. Their leap of faith, in purchasing farm land in the 1920s, demonstrated to me their desire to make a good living.

Many life lessons and truths were taught to me be my grandparents. Some of these were as follows:

1. Self-reliance: Many of the staples we needed to eat were grown on the farm.

2. Saving: Grandma Mamie had a formula for getting rich. She suggested saving 15 cents out of every dollar earned. Coins from the summer events on the Pavillion were saved in Prince Albert Tobacco cans and were counted during the winter months.

3. Preservation: Before there was a Green Movement, the Derricks were recycling and fallowing the fields.

4. Family: Members of the family were very protective of the children. We were very sheltered and only played with selected children and family members in our age group.

5. Friendship: One of my grandmother's friends was Mrs. "Sweet" Louis Bing Roberts. She rode the city bus from Wheaton Street to 617 Park Avenue to pick me up for Sunday School every Sunday.

6. Spirituality: Two churches that helped to formulate my values were First African Baptist and Mount Zion Second Baptist. My grandfather, Joe Derrick, was a Baptist Minister of the Gospel.

Savannah and Derrick's Inn were filled with memories that have taken me through life. When I entered elementary school I attended George W. DeRenne. My aunt, Laura Derrick Webb, taught there. I rode with her to school daily. Mrs. Virginia Kiah was my art teacher at Alfred E. Beach Junior High School. I visited her home/museum on West 36th Street often. It was filled with art work and flowers. As I matured, I began to visit my family in Atlanta. Eventually, I moved there during my high school years. I attended Turner High School. Mrs. Isabella Tobin was my English teacher/counselor. Ironically, her husband, Rev. Lucius Tobin, served as the pastor of the church my mother attended—Providence Baptist Church (now Providence Missionary Baptist Church).

617 Park Avenue was my family's city home. It was built by my aunt, Miss. Mary E. F. Burns, a prominent educator in Savannah. Former business owner/mortician Frank Bynes, Sr., often spoke of her rigid gait and snow white hair. My cousin, Helen Fletcher Scroggins, played on the sidewalk of this home with me causing havoc to those who walked by. No other home in the neighborhood had a sidewalk. Neighbors weren't allowed to walk on the sidewalk. Keep in mind Park Avenue hadn't been paved.

At Derrick's Inn my Aunt Laura was the keeper of the animals. She loved those animals—cows, pigs, geese, ducks, dogs, chickens. Pal, the pony, was my birthday present when I turned ten; and Jack the mule was my grandfather's work mule. Pal was a pet but somewhat wild. There was a rooster named Bull Connor who was my baby sitter. Each time I would leave the porch at Derrick's Inn, the rooster would chase me; a great disciplinarian.

On March 2, 2012, my brother, Ronald (Ronnie) died after a long illness. I became very close to him towards the end of his life. Peggy, a close friend of Ronnie's, was very attentive to him towards the end of his life. My cousin, Rev. Matthew Southall Brown, Jr., was also attentive to Ronnie. He "Walked Him Back to Christ." For this I am thankful. Through his death, he will be united with our ancestors:

Samuel Brown

William Brown

Lydia Burns

Jane Burns Brown (Great Grandmother)

Joseph Brown

Mamie Brown Derrick (Grandmother)

Joseph William Derrick (Grandfather)

Rosa Brown

Albert B. Cameron, Sr. (Father)

Clarence Brown

Jennie (Janie) Brown

Christopher Brown

Willie Brown

Sarah Brown

Laura Brown

Nathaniel Brown

Mollie D. Cameron (Mother)

Thanks to the Burns, Browns, Derricks, and Cameron families for what they instilled in me.

Albert Benjamin Cameron, Jr.

My Road to the Institute
Reflections on an Unbelievable Awakening, Journey and Experience
Derrick's Inn
Joseph Miller

Upon reflecting, it appears that the idea had its origin one early winter evening in 1955. Together with my two brothers, I had been relocated to Savannah, Georgia two years earlier almost immediately following my mother's death to live with members of her family. My older brother preferred life in the city but I shared space with my younger brother at Aunt Mamie's house in the 'country' as I liked to refer to the multi-acre compound, eponymously called Derrick's Inn by those outside of the family that she and my Uncle Joseph W. Derrick, years prior, had established eight miles south of the city.

As I sat on a huge wood desk while completing my ninth grade homework, I was unprepared for what was soon to emerge and how my life would be altered as a result. In spite of the periodic crackles from the wood burning in the fireplace, and the constant conversation—some seemingly commencing randomly and then some brief and with abrupt endings, and others that were either continuations from days past and still others that seemed purposely initiated to move forward reluctantly with endings that lacked definition—among one or more of the congregants, I managed each evening to happily and productively engage my school assignments. But that evening was going to be special. In fact, for me it would be pivotal. The conversation that was about to occur with one of my aunts would leave what might be described as an indelible impression on my conscious.

When asked by one of my aunts whether I liked my algebra course, I responded by stating that I was truly fascinated by the combination of literal expressions with numerical ones. I continued by remarking that it was clear to me that a facility with mathematics was a requirement for the successful study of engineering. And, studying engineering was my plan. Years before, I conveyed I selected 'Georgia Tech'—as it was referred to although formally it was Georgia Institute of Technology—as my college choice, and I was doing all that I could to prepare for my acceptance there. When I finished speaking not one of the five or six adults that were present uttered a solitary word. After a few minutes passed, I inquired as to why everyone had become silent. Not surprisingly, outspoken Sarah

Jeanette Derrick Herring (Aunt Jeanette) a recent college graduate, and now an elementary school teacher, informed me that I should perhaps investigate MIT because 'Georgia Tech' did not admit Negroes to study there.

Did not admit Negroes? Although I knew what that meant, I did not understand why Negroes were not allowed admission. And, I was reluctant to inquire perhaps because I didn't choose to once again be informed that White people believed Negroes to be inferior and similarly treated them. Perhaps I didn't want to mentalize about how my skin color, nappy hair and other Negroid features made me different from the majority of people.

Perhaps I chose not at the time to recall how seemingly many of my White classmates and teachers in Astoria Queens, New York relished singing "Old Black Joe" during class and at assembly programs, while cognizant that I, Joseph R Miller, was the only Negro person in the entire school building. Perhaps, I didn't want to surface thoughts of limits. So, I decided to drown myself in the letters MIT.

MIT? To what was she referring? I had not heard of MIT. Immediately clued in to my seeming unfamiliarity, Aunt Jeanette politely conveyed that MIT refers to the Massachusetts Institute of Technology. Among its pluses she said is its support to Negroes who are interested in science, mathematics, and engineering; its proximity to New York was of interest to me because I was born in New York, and lived there until 1953; and its more prestigious reputation than engineering school in the country because of its faculty, research, and its challenging curricula. "Does it have football," I asked. She replied that she did not know but in her opinion that should not be a determinant for me. In my silent and teenage manner I forgave her for being still another woman who failed to understand the importance of sports to the human condition.

That night, after the lights were dimmed and I lay prostrate, I spent a fair amount of time thinking about college and, more specifically, considering MIT. There was much to ponder; including its distance from Savannah, and related transportation costs; my younger brother's existence without a big brother around; tuition; room and board; books; scholarship money. There too existed surfacing, perhaps for the first time in my life, a fear of failure. Suppose the scholarship from

General Electric, General Motors or from AT&T didn't come through? What would I do if Phillip didn't want me to leave him alone in Savannah? What if my high school grades were to sag and/or I failed to obtain adequate recommendations from my teachers? Would I disappoint my highly revered Uncle Joe, Aunt Mamie's husband, if I were to be accepted, enrolled and later I graduated?

In two short years Uncle Joseph W. Derrick was able to exert more influence over my life than had any male figure. A real man, father, uncle, brother-in-law, teacher, preacher, friend, neighbor; he desired that all male children in the family become lawyers. And, after being successful at that vocation, it was his wish that they would 'receive the call' and head to the ministry. Although I would not want to disappoint him, I knew too that he was one person who could and would understand a man following his dream; and especially so if by so doing it brought credit upon himself and his family.

Well, I failed to make the cut from high school to MIT. By the time I reached my senior year at the Haaren High School, after returning to New York, I realized that although I enjoyed mathematics, and was engaged by its challenges, unless I received lots of support from my teachers, my skills with the subject would be insufficient for adequate preparation as an engineer. Although I had to initiate an alternative plan, and despite this veering from course, MIT remained prominent in my designs for my future.

High school graduation came and my schedule changed from a thirty hour work week to that of a forty hour work week and daily visits to Haaren High School. With graduation from high school came other adjustments as well. Among them were my relocation from closet and cot, community showers and the piercing observations of me by the homosexual group with whom I shared living arrangements at the Harlem YMCA, as well as full responsibility for my younger brother. However, it took only a short three years of being employed first as a rack boy in the garment district, next as a messenger, and later as a clerk, together with the aforementioned responsibility, for me to determine that the only way for me to reach my career goals was to return to school. With that in mind, I decided to take advantage of the scholarship program offered by the City of New York. My application to and enrollment at the College of the City of New York soon followed, although I continued full-time employment Monday through Friday, and I maintained a part-time job at St. Vincent's Hospital on weekends.

Yes, it was much less than easy for me. At the time, the College of the City of New York offered one of the most academically demanding undergraduate programs in the nation. My journey in search of a major took me down a winding road from accounting to political science to industrial psychology. Once in the world of vocational psychology, experimental psychology and psychometrics, I knew that my interests were satisfied. And, the productivity studies conducted at Western Electric together with Taylor's Scientific Management Theory caught my attention and to this day I remain profoundly interested in both approaches to operations management as well as to the ancillary behavioral issues.

Three and one-half years later I exited CCNY with an undergraduate degree. Needless to say, I did not graduate cum laude. And although I had not connected with MIT, its existence was now more prominently known to me than ever. I wanted more than ever to be a student on its campus. Perhaps I now have it all wrong but it seemed that I was nagged by a belief that I had made a MIT commitment to my family in Georgia and it seemed that I had failed to meet that commitment. Oh well, I still had time to do something at MIT.

Private industry entry level jobs for college educated Negroes were for the most part unavailable at the time. Much like my cohorts, I took a civil service examination and was hired by the City of New York as a case worker in its Department of Social Services. I enrolled in graduate level evening courses at CCNY. All of this while Phillip, my younger brother who lived with me, was a junior in high school and was preparing for a successful and fun-filled senior year; while I was readying myself for work as a social work professional.

Approaching my responsibilities at my place of employment, in the manner that was for me characteristic, proved difficult. Surrounded by an educated class of people, some my age and others slightly older, my expectations were disappointed. Although the mission was an honorable one, social work case management, as practiced by New York City government, seemed to me to be only a tad better than what one would have expected at the time in the USSR. And my colleagues, be mindful that they were largely self-admitted 'do gooders,' largely between twenty-five and thirty years old; and in the middle decades of the sixties, seemed more self absorbed than concerned about their clients, their employment and their careers. For the most part they were immersed in 'live and let live,' sex, drugs, and 'rock and roll' and I was in awe of all of it.

It was a very good year, indeed. Phillip was an almost perfect younger brother at school, after school and at home. There was much for me to learn at work, during and after work with my colleagues, and in the quietude of my personal space. I soon became able to evaluate welfare families apart from my personal experiences with the system and I was happily as well as sadly surprised by the findings of this social dynamic. For the most part I was afforded my first shot at romantic relationships. All were of a deliberate transient construction, and for whatever are the reasons, were maintained as such. Phillip and I had sufficient clothing and food and a little entertainment money for the first time since my mom had died; and we occupied a fairly nice one bedroom apartment facing a scenic well maintained Crotona Park in the Bronx, New York.

Then out of the blue, and perhaps not, I received that expected but less than desirable large envelop from my local Selective Service Board. After much back and forth discussion with members of the Board about my physical readiness for military duty, I was deemed qualified. By now Phillip had completed high school, had obtained a full-time job and was enrolled in an evening program at one of the local community colleges. When the "Greetings" letter arrived, Phillip was the first person whom I informed. After explaining that I had only three weeks remaining as a civilian, he, unbeknownst to me, immediately sought 'refuge' in the United States Marine Corps by enlisting and receiving an almost certain experience in the Republic of Viet-Nam.

Two weeks later he had severed employment, canceled his courses and I was on the subway accompanying him to Fort Hamilton in Brooklyn, New York for his induction. Four days later I was scheduled to appear at Whitehall Street for my induction into the United States Army. And so it occurred, commencing with Fort Jackson, South Carolina then Fort Gordon, Georgia; followed by Fort McClellan, Alabama for advanced Infantry Training. Surely I would never get to MIT, I thought.

After AIT, I detoured to Officer Candidate School at Fort Sill's Artillery and Missile School. Artillery and missiles? What are they I thought? My OSC preference had been the Finance Corps and the Quartermaster Corps. Did my mathematics scores have something to do with my placement among the combat corps? Twenty-four weeks later, I was in the best physical condition and the best mental condition of my life and I asked my dear friend and fellow candidate while in OCS, John Scherrill (he was killed before completing sixty days in Viet-Nam) to affix my lieutenant bars after his wife affixed his bars.

By now Phillip was in Viet-Nam. He was stationed near the demilitarized zone with a Marine infantry unit. My graduating military orders read 'deployed to Southern Asia.' I was transferred to Fort Dix to await further orders. While there I volunteered for Ranger School and I was immediately dispatched for Fort Benning, Georgia where in no time at all I became very familiar with the Harmony Church area of the vast military reservation. Upon returning to Fort Dix, I was made a permanent party and never again did I hear anything about South Vietnam and surely I was careful not to inquire.

Over the next several months, thoughts of graduate school and the GI Bill began to surface. Would MIT accept me? Could I 'cut it' at MIT? How would I pay the tuition?

By the time I had completed my military obligation, much had changed in the civilian world of work. For the first time young college educated African-American males were being considered for entry level positions in the private sector. All who were veterans, regardless of race and ethnicity, were given some priority and seemingly those who had been officers were awarded preference above all others. After many interviews and several with the same potential employers, I chose Citibank and its management training program.

Five years and several promotions later, it was eminently clear to me that to truly compete for the top spots at Citicorp, and for that matter most other businesses one needed amongst other things a graduate degree in either a business subject or an engineering related topic. From financial services to transportation to bio-tech to communications to engineering and beyond, one appeared to be limiting oneself if one's portfolio was absent a graduate degree. I enrolled in graduate school as a preparatory measure. I set my sights on business school a Columbia University, Harvard University, and the University of Pennsylvania; but during the process of submitting applications my supervisor—younger than me, taller than me, White male with a Master of Business Administration degree and earning annually about seventy-five thousand dollars more than me not including bonuses, stock grants, and stock options—suggested that I consider the Sloan School of Management.

Where is and what is the Sloan School of Management? Why the Sloan School? With just a wee bit of investigatory effort I learned the answers to my questions. I had for years considered MIT to be solely an educational institution for those interested in science, engineering, and mathematics. I soon learned that the business school sign is misleading. Yes, the business school too is about science, engineering and mathematics.

Although I continued on my way with the other universities, I took my supervisor's advice. After testing, an application, recommendations and interviews, I was accepted for admission to 'The Institute' as it is referred to by its students, administration, faculty and proud graduates. Finally, I was in but little did I know what an academic challenge it would be for me. After taking a leave of absence from my place of employment, I spent the first two semesters in Cambridge, Massachusetts doing absolutely nothing except attending classes, discussing assignments, reading business strategy with my professors and studying. I required tutoring in mathematics. I required an attitude change about the importance of marketing. I was offered assistance with my communication skills. My social skills were ripe for upgrade and they too didn't go unaddressed.

During this time several relationships were ended and one in particular devastated me. My lady friend of several years apparently found a better opportunity and she aggressively took advantage of it. I was…

There were occasions when I was ready to give up. There were times when I felt that I was unsuited for this educational experience. There were more than one event when I required and respectfully demanded the time of Phyllis A. Wallace, Ph.D. (first African American to obtain tenure at MIT) in an effort to get me back on track and in spite of her busy teaching, research, consulting, and community work schedules, she always willingly cooperated. For me, the experience at

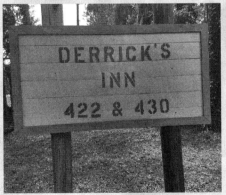

'The Institute' was strangely similar to that at Fort Sill. Both had a way of humbling even the mightiest.

By way of an example, the top score on our first mathematics examination was 79 (seventy-nine) followed by 68 (sixty-eight) and the lowest score was 21 (twenty-one). I scored a pitiful 59 (fifty-nine). Both relieved and disappointed, I pondered whether I should take advantage of the make-up examination. Based upon the scoring curve I would receive a passing grade, but as far as I was concerned, I had failed; and failing was not something that I would accept for myself. However, failing 'make-up' meant one had to begin again the course. Mind you, we had five doctoral degree holders—two in mathematics and three in engineering—in my business school class. Only five—I was one of them—among us failed to have either a Master of Arts or a Master of Science degree. I soon learned that if I were not among the brightest folks in the world, then certainly I was among some of the brightest. I decided to accept the grade I was given and skip the 'make-up' test. Wrong! Those who took the 'make-up' examination remarked that it was much less difficult than the original one.

Perhaps it's true, Being There terms the struggle, did come to a satisfying end. I completed my coursework, had my graduate paper accepted by my adviser and I enthusiastically defended it before the thesis committee. About ten days later, I was awarded a Master of Science degree from Massachusetts Institute of Technology.

I was enormously proud⊠as were my two brothers. Uncle Joe was now deceased; and although I had neither become a lawyer nor a preacher, it was under his roof that I became aware of 'The Institute' and for my family I had sort of made history. I wanted him to be proud of my accomplishment. I too want Aunt Jeanette and her sisters—Aunt Laura and Aunt Molly—and their mother, Aunt Mamie to be proud; and so I promptly informed them of my achievement.

After petitioning for re-entry, I returned to Citibank, although my sense several years later was that graduation from MIT would have been an auspicious time for me to take advantage of some of the offers that were at the time presented to me. Despite the uncomfortable first few months, I was eventually offered a great assignment and within one year of returning I was promoted to the level of Vice President. Notable at the time was that there were less than a half dozen Black Vice Presidents in

major banks around the United States of America—and I was
one of them.

The MIT experience and degree have stood me in good stead
wherever I have managed to roam professionally as well as personally. I
am grateful to my mother's family for all that they did to make the dream
for me a reality.

Yes, dreams can come true if one relentlessly pursues them, and if
one is able to meet the challenges of those dreams. In closing and in the
words of Henry Ford, I submit the following: "Whether you believe that
you can or that you cannot, in either case you are right."

Cousin Joe died September 2, 2015 in Nashville, Tennessee, at
12:40 a.m.

Remembering My Cousin At
120 Westminster Street
LaTia M. Brown McDaniels

As the scent from the plethora of fried ocean delights filled the
house, Daddy would begin to close off the kitchen. "Dot, I don't want
this fried grease smell filling the house. It gets all down in your clothes ya
know." With an apparent glare of offense she sucks her teeth,
murmurs something and continues cooking while singing Negro
spirituals. Leighanna and Leah begin gathering their various activities to
occupy Aunt Chris and me. Well, I usually vacuum and pick up around
the house chuckling at the complaints and retorts bellowing back and
forth from Ma and Dad.

Minutes later Honk, HOOOONK, a car pulls up with a gold tag
that has "Pastor Brown" on it. The girls begin to frantically dash around
the house simultaneously yelling "They're here!" I stand at the door
waiting to see who is going to come out of the car (because you never
now). Even Sheppard, our dog, seems to be aware of the gathering that is
about to take place, so he paces until his excitement is broken. "Sheppard,
out of my house!" Ma never liked him around the food or in the
dining room. As I hold the door open, Grandpa and Grandma, Aunt
Chris and Cousin Ronnie enter the house smiling faces and various
greetings to everyone in the house. Grandma, who is always the first in

the house, quickly states her displeasure with the temperature. "Dot, it smells good in here, but it's cold." Astonished and obviously overheated, Ma reluctantly walks down the hallway to turn the air off and replies, "Mother, you're hot? It's 72 outside and 78 inside." Ma was pretty big on respect when it came to my grandparents, even if it was at the expense of her own comfort.

Cousin Ronnie, usually the last one in the house, would come in with a brief case in his hand and a bottle of juice in the other. "Cousin Ronnie!!!!!!!" Leighana and Leah zip pass everyone to jump in his arms. At the top of her lungs Leighanna begis telling her Cousin Ronnie a conglomeration of second grade stories as she leads him to the brown recliner in the living room. Leah follows behind with a game that almost weighs as much as she does, "Play, Playyyyyyyyy!," she pleads trying to drown out Leighana's ongoing stories. Unable to win the yelling war, she sits with her Cousin and studies him patiently; waiting for him to acknowledge her and the game she wanted to play. Aunt Chris comes to diffuse the attention situation. "Come on Leah," she says. Aunt Chris was like a walking songbird. She seemed to never stop singing. It was like a constant secret testimony to God. As I try to quiet Leighana and her story that has reached its seven minute mark, Cousin Ronnie requests the remote. "How do you work this thing? The game is on." Even though he was no stranger to my parents' house (or television) he would always seem to forget how to operate the remote control. Funny thing is I never knew what channel ESPN was on so I would just randomly push three numbers and hope it would be close to his desired channel. After the television watched him for a little while, the announcement that everyone had been waiting for was made, "Dinner is ready"

An array of food filled the large mahogany table. Fried whiting, boiled corn, dinner rolls, boiled shrimp and fried shrimp, potato salad, stuffed flounder, and a fresh salad barely allowed room for the plates and glasses. "Mariah, get some ice." Since I can't cook, Ma always placed me in charge of ice and taste testing. I didn't mind and I am sure no one else did either. There we all were at the table as a family. After the food was blessed, silence blanketed the table and servings were piled onto plates. I sat back patiently waiting my turn. It was taboo to fix food before ANY family member older than myself. It was a rule placed in the imaginary book of the Brown family's do's and don'ts. I would only get a little bit of food, that way I could spend less time eating and more time listening to comical stories. As the food portions diminished, somehow the conversation would settle around Daddy's church. "Remember that time you got a finger cross pressed on your forehead by the crazy lady?" Ma always seemed to be the initiator of funny church stories. Cousin Ronnie belts out a laugh that still echoes in my head now. He had a way of making things that really weren't all that funny hilarious simply because of his contagious laugh. He animated tales of fishing, heartbreaking tales of malice, and an engaging story of redemption make me miss him as I sit here looking at the dinner table tonight. When Leah slowly walked over to me and whispered, "Where is Cousin Ronnie?" I just hugged her and vowed to never take another moment or family for granted. Life is extremely precious and that is one of the reasons why I call to check on you (Grandpa) and Grandma. I don't want to waste another day not knowing how the two of you are doing. A week is entirely too long to go without checking on you or any family member.

I wrote all of this just to say I LOVE YOU GUYS, AND I CHERISH EVERY MOMENT WE SPEND TOGETHER AS A FAMILY. Let's not forget about each other nor the time spent with one another for granted.

Ronald Cameron died March 2, 2012.

XII

THE SOUTH CAROLINA SEA ISLANDS

"Bin Yah-Cum Yah"
The South Carolina Sea Islands

"Eb ry ting chan gin up down ya" was a documentary that explained the plight of an old Gullah woman living on Hilton Head Island. The narrator asked her, "Do you realize you are living below the poverty line?" Her response was, "Eb ry ting I need come from da grun. I ain't no I be po til yo tell me. Eb ry ting chan gin up down ya."

The history of Hilton Head Island dates back to 10,000 to 15,000 BC, when the paleo-Indians explored the Low Country. The Archaic Period, 8,000-2,000 BC saw the Woodland Indians living on the Island. They lived here seasonally on the bounty of the waterways.

The written history of Hilton Head Island began with the Spaniards in 1526, as they explored the coastal waters from Key West, Florida to the St. Lawrence River in Canada. They called this territory "LA Florida."

Captain Jean Ribaut (Ribault), a French Huguenot led this Protestant religious group to Hilton Head Island in 1562. Under his leadership a fort was built. It was named Port Royal, near the present town of Port Royal, located in Beaufort County, South Carolina.

In 1663, Captain William Hilton identified headlands near the entrance of Port Royal Sound. He named it Hilton's Head, in honor of himself. The word 'Head' refers to the headlands visible to his expedition as they sailed the unchartered waters. He lingered several days, making notes of the trees, crops, sweet water and the sweet air.

The African American presence on the island of Hilton Head has its origins in slavery. The Africans developed a unique culture based on language, religion, folklore, and spiritual redemption. This culture is referred to as 'The Gullah Culture.' The word 'Gullah' is believed to have derived from an African tribe called the Gola. They were found along the borders of Sierra Leone and West Africa. "The survival of African people away from their ancestral home is one of the greatest acts of human endurance in the history of the world," states Dr. John Henrick Clark.

When the Union Troops took over Hilton Head Island during the Civil

War (1861-1865), hundreds of ex-slaves flocked to the Island. They were the descendents of early Gullah People. Mitchelville was the first township established for freedmen. Established in 1862, it was named for Ormsby M. Mitchel, a Union Army general. Mitchelville was called the "Port Royal Experiment." This experiment was enacted to prepare newly freed slaves for democratic participation post Civil War. The towns people elected their own officials and passed their own laws.

While teaching in Spartanburg District 7, South Carolina, in 1974, I taught ninth grade students at Evans Junior High School. The class consisted of predominantly Caucasian students. A young female student named Bailey gave me a copy of the book The Water Is Wide by Pat Conroy. This book told the eye opening and challenging teaching experiences Conroy had while teaching on Daufuskie Island. This island is a sea island found between Hilton Head and the mainland of Beaufort, South Carolina. Many Savannahians remember the river excursions to Daufuskie Island on Captain Sam Steven's boat, The Waving Girl. The Gullah inhabitants of the island sold their fresh seafood to the trip's participants.

Fast forward to the year 2007.... I was in the process of moving to Beaufort, South Carolina to teach. An interview had been scheduled for me at Hilton Head High School. A middle aged coach was the interviewer. He quickly informed me that I wouldn't be able to afford to live on the island. He made this assumption. Needless to say, I wasn't assigned to this school. Ironically, approximately fifty years earlier, my family would vacation in the home of Mrs. Nancy Walker and her sister, Mrs. Stewart. Their home was on Bradley Beach, found on Hilton Head Island.

I agree with the old Gullah woman, "eb ry ting chaii giii up down ya."

Analyzing the data relative to Hilton Head Island, it seems to be a "Tale of Two Cities."

Population – African American   2,758 (8.1%)
    White   26,752 (79%)
    Asian   181 (0.5%)
    Hispanic   3,886 (11.5%)
    Two or More Races   246 (0.2%)

Land Area   42.1 Square Miles
Population Density   814 People Per Square Mile
Unemployment Rates – Hilton Head   5.9%
 South Carolina   10.3%
Average Household Size   2.3 People
Percentage of Family Households   68.7%
Percentage of Households with Unmarried Partners   3.5%
Residents Below Poverty Level   7.3%
Residents with Income Below 50% of the Poverty Level   3.3%
Most Common Industries of Males Construction
Most Common Industries for Women   Accommodations, Food
Service, Health Care

The South Carolina Sea Islands
Anita Singleton Prather

Gullah and Geechee, gumbo and collards. Who would have thought 25 years ago that Gullah today would be such a sought after phenomenon—researched by scholars from around the world, movie directors, tour operators, and many more? This unique and rich cultural birth, in the American South, born of the Triangular Trans-Atlantic Slave Trade, was looked upon with much ridicule, shame and deep pain.

Located on the Sea Islands of South Carolina and Georgia are communities of people who are descendants of enslaved Africans. They have a rich heritage linked to the West African rice cultivating countries such as Sierra Leone, Angola, Liberia, Senegal, Ivory Coast, Guinea and others. In South Carolina, this group of African Americans and the language they speak is referred to as Gullah. On the Georgia side, they are called Geechee. Another term to refer to these descendants are Native Islanders.

Some historians believe that the word "Gullah" comes from Angola or maybe from Gola, a tribal name found near the border of Liberia and Sierra Leone in West Africa. The word "Geechee" could have originated from the mis-pronunciation of the tribal name of Kissi from Sierra Leone. The exact origin of these names is not known, but most agree that the Gullah people and their language are African based.

During the late 1960s, European settlers in the new American colonies needed more workers to cultivate thousands of acres of land on their sea island plantations. The masters of these plantations had attempted to use Native Americans as slaves but had very little success.

Many West Africans were skilled master cultivators and builders. Plantation masters wanted people from regions that were skilled in indigo, rice, and cotton cultivation. Rice, a crop that Africans had mastered for centuries, was highly desired throughout the world. By 1700, "Carolina Golden Rice," as it was called, became a major export from the Sea Islands. It brought great wealth to the plantation aristocrats.

The climate of the Carolina coastline was very similar to that of the coast of West Africa. The Portuguese were the first Europeans to realize the profit in human cargo and so began the importation of millions of Africans to America carried by European ships. The Middle Passage voyage started on the coast of West Africa then proceeded down to the West Indies with the point of entry being the east coast of America. The largest percentage (75%) entering America came through the ports of Georgetown, Charleston, and Beaufort, South Carolina.

Gullah is the blending of the cultures of the West Africans who were the enslaved workers on these plantations, with that of the Europeans who became the masters; and that of the Native Americans who were the original landowners. It is the unique blend of the West African culture, combined with European and Native American influences of all the different languages, food ways, religious practices, crafts, music and traditions resulting in this distinct culture that is known today as Gullah.

Out of the ashes of America's Civil War, this West African based heritage survived along the east coast of the Carolinas, Georgia, Northern Florida, and out west in parts of Texas and Oklahoma. There are even Gullah speaking communities in Mexico, the Caribbean and the Caicos, and the Turks Islands.

Growing up on the Sea Islands of Beaufort, South Carolina was a time characterized by a slower pace—almost as if time was standing still. I cherish the memories of close family ties, gatherings, respect for your elders, Decoration Day (May 30th), all day crabbing outings, fresh vegetables from my Grandma's garden, Sunday church services, and

James Dawson, Sr. (1835-1920) - 1st generation

This man is the earliest documented patriarch of the Dawson line. He, apparently, lived in slavery in South Carolina, but also fought for freedom as a private during the U.S. Civil War (USCT-SC-33rd Regiment). He married a woman named Judy [maiden name unknown] (1845- ?) and they had 13 children (Sophie, George, James Jr., Lydia, Laura, Grace, Julia, Maria, William, Hattie, Peter, Sarah & unknown). He later married Rebecca Grant (1854-1923), though they did not have children. To date, I have not been able to document James Dawson's parents.

draft-2018.1

Judy [maiden name?] (1845-?) - 1st generation

I have not been able to document Judy's parents or the exact date of her death. According to the 1900 U.S. Census, she gave birth to 13 children, though only 11 were living. She was living in the same household as her husband James Dawson Sr. in Sheldon County, Beaufort, South Carolina-most likely what is known as Dale, SC. Children listed in the household at that time included (James Jr., Maria, William, Hattie, Peter and Sarah). Judy's parents were reported to have been born in South Carolina. In the 1910 U.S. Census, Rebecca-not Judy-was listed as the wife of James Dawson Sr. Judy's disposition(death, divorce, etc.) is-hitherto- unknown.

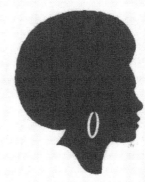

draft-2018.1

James Dawson, Jr. (1869-1923) - 2nd generation

Son of James Dawson, Sr (1835-1920) and Judy [maiden name?] Dawson. (1845-?).

Husband of Lucille [Knowles] Dawson(18??-?).

Father to James "Gussie"(1905-1962).

Compiled By Donald Jackson

Aunt Sophie Daise of St. Helena Island
Sophisticated Ladies of yester years.

George Dawson, Sr. (1864- ?) - 2nd generation

Son of James Dawson, Sr (1835-1920) and
Judy [maiden name?] Dawson. (1845-?).

Husband of Celia [Heywood] Dawson
(1868-1929).

Father to Lottie(1889-1920), Bessie(1891-?),
George, Jr.(1892-?), John(1894-?), Francis
(1899-?) and Reginia Irene(1906-1953).

family dinners in the country. I could not see through my young eyes, the treasure of wealth I had growing up here in the late 1950s.

Unlike so many Gullahs in my community, we were not taught to be ashame of our culture. We were not allowed to make fun of the elders or others talking that so called 'funny talk' or 'bad language.' My parents, especially my Grandmother Rosa Singleton—the real 'Pearlie Sue'—were very proud people who instilled in me and my siblings that same sense of pride and dignity in our culture. At those Sunday dinners I would sit quietly listening attentively, mesmerized by the rhythmic tongues of my elders telling stories of the 'good old days.' Not even in my wildest dream would I have imagined I would be passing the torch to the next generation and to the world.

Dawson Family Connection

Gullah is the umbilical cord that connects us all to the womb of Mother Africa; the Cradle of all Civilization. Gullah is not a 'Me Ting,' but a 'We Ting.'

Hey cousin, we be family. We is all Gullah Kinfolk.
Hab'yahsef a Gullah good time. Yah year me!
The Dawson Family Connection
The South Carolina Sea Islands
(Beaches, Islands, Family)
Leonard Brown

South Carolina holds a special place in my heart. My mother's mother, Regina Dawson, hails from Seabrook, South Carolina. Her husband, my grandfather, Edward Williams, Sr., is from Grey's Hill, South Carolina. My father's mother, Helen Robinson, is from Columbia, South Carolina. His father, Christopher Brown's family, traces their roots to the White Hall Plantation in Colleton County, South Carolina.

As a young child, I remember our trips to the beaches on the coast of South Carolina. Prominent African American Savannahnians had purchased beach property on Hilton Head Island. These beaches bore the names of its owners. One example of this ownership was Collier Beach. Dr. and Mrs. Henry Collier, Jr. owned and built a house on this strip of beach which had his name. On Bradley Beach, Mrs. Nancy H. Walker and her sister, Mrs. Stewart, owned a beach house. They would allow my family to stay at their house during the summer months. Other owners of houses and land were Mr. and Mrs. George Washington, the Laws, and Dr. And Mrs. Kiah. Today some of these properties can't be recognized or accessed. The most recognizable area to me is Bradley Beach Road.

Hunting Island, South Carolina is a state park. It was a place where African Americans could visit in the 1960s. It was and still is almost a deserted stretch of beach. On one occasion, my father spotted a puddle of fish caught at low tide. He reached in the puddle to grab one fish that was jumping and fell straight to the bottom. The puddle must have been several feet deep. We thought he had drowned. Being that he was a good swimmer, he popped to the surface. Hunting Island was and is beautiful, yet dangerous.

St. Helena Island, South Carolina holds spiritual and religious memories. My father, Rev. Matthew Southall Brown, Sr., had a very good friend in the ministry. His name was Rev. Price. He pastored Brick Baptist Church. Brick was built by slaves in 1855. The balcony was reserved for the slaves to stand during the services. In 1861 the church was turned over to freed slaves at the beginning of the Civil War. We often traveled to the island to worship with Rev. Price and his family. I often heard my father speaking with Dr. Blanton Black who also pastored on the island. His church was entitled St. Joseph (Bethesda). Ironically, Rev. Black was my geography instructor at Savannah State College (SSU). His family lived on our street in Savannah, Georgia. The street was Victory Drive. Finally, my father had an interest in pastoring either St. James or Faith Memorial Baptist Church. As a child, I remember these churches being without air conditioning and filled with gnats. My siblings and I pleaded with my father not to accept a call from this church, if it came. It never came.

Daufuskie Island was the final destination of Captain Sam Stevens' river cruise up the Savannah River. Captain Stevens owned and operated a pleasure boat called the 'Waving Girl.' Different social and religious groups in Savannah would book the use of his boat as fundraisers. The cruise would take its travelers to Daufuskie. The inhabitants of the island would have fresh cooked and raw seafood for sale. After a stay on the island, the travelers would board the boat and take a nice slow trip down the river back to Savannah. Several years ago a member of the Hudson family in Savannah, Mrs. Brown donated ten acres of land on Daufuskie to St. John Baptist Church. It was instructed by the family that the land was to be developed. If it wasn't, it would be returned to the family. What became of this land, God only knows.

While living in Beaufort, South Carolina during the years of 2007-2009, I hoped to connect with my mother's family, the Dawsons. I observed a difference in the people and the culture of the islands. The warm, friendly and easy going lifestyle had shifted. It shifted to scenes of gated communities, international tourists, yacht clubs, gated beaches and pockets of African-American communities. I was searching for the Beaufort of my youth, which may never return. However, there are people and organizations that are trying to preserve the Gullah Culture—i.e. The Gullah Festival, Anita Singleton Prather, Marquetta Goodwine, Ronald Daise, Representative James Clyburn, Marlina Smalls, Emory Campbell, Louise Cohen, Joe Opala, The Gullah/Geechee Cultural Heritage Corridor and The Gullah Kinfolks.

Quoting and old Gullah inhabitant of Edisto Island, "Everything Change Up Now."

Liberty Hill
North Charleston, South Carolina
Rev. Matthew Southall Brown, Jr.

From 1962 to 1969 our family experienced an African-American community that would impact our lives forever. This community was located in North Charleston, South Carolina. It was called Liberty Hill. A small church, Royal Baptist, had called my father, Rev. Matthew Southall Brown, Sr., as their pastor. I was only eight years old. For seven years we were a traveling family; packing on Friday afternoon and taking a two and a half hour drive to North Charleston, South Carolina.

Upon our arrival in Charleston, the church had arranged for us to live with Deacon and Mrs. Charlie Sanders. The Sanders had a modest yet clean home. Eight people lived under their roof Friday through Sunday: my parents, my siblings and the Sanders. There were two bedrooms and one bathroom. Their home was located in a small compound. The Dinkins, Olivers and Richardsons had small homes in this fenced compound. Two young people around our ages lived in the compound. They were Stevie Oliver and Gwendolyn Dinkins. We often watched scary movies late at night with them—The Twilight Zone, I believe. We ate lots of beef stew and rice at the Sander's home. It was delicious. The sweets were also good. However, we had to watch out for chewing tobacco in the drinking glasses. Mrs. Sanders chewed tobacco.

I met many friends on Liberty Hill. I would say Phil Ellison was my best friend. Phil Ellison and I did a lot of exploring of Liberty Hill. Much of it was done by foot. We saw some amazing things for our ages— people living underground, and rats living in ditches. We used the rats as target practice with our BB guns. Liberty Hill was a depressed area but it was clean. At one point, we ran across a drunken man shooting a gun in the air. Phil grabbed me and pulled me down to protect me…what a friend!

I often spent the night at Randolph Jenkins' home. His parents, Deacon Frank and Annie May Jenkins, had a very nice home. It was located north of Liberty Hill, off Highway 291. Randolph, my brother, and I would go bike riding. These trips were fun but when I look back they were very dangerous. We rode our bikes on Interstate 26!! It seemed as though we were literally traveling 50 miles per hour. I was scared. I remember Randolph giving me his BB gun to kill a chicken that he called a problem. It was the first thing I ever killed. I was sick to my stomach.

There was a mulatto family that lived in Andrews, South Carolina. They were the Harper family. I believe there were eight children. The children I remember were Reggie, Bernard, Karen, Rosie and Tony. Their father owned a Phillips 66 service station on Highway 291. Each of my siblings called themselves dating the four older Harper children; in this order: Bernard and Maxine, Reggie and Christa, Leonard and Karen, Matthew and Rosie. I clearly remember Rosie dumping me. I was in love with her. I cried very hard over the breakup. To let me down easy, she sent me the song, "Love Potion No 9." It didn't work.

The church services at Royal Baptist were scary to me. There was lots of clapping, stomping and shouting. We weren't accustomed to this type of worship service. Having come from First African Baptist in Savannah, Georgia, this type of worship was foreign to us. There was a young lady named Jean. I remember Jean shouting and rolling on the floor, all the while she had her baby in her arms. Mother Bradshaw, the elder of the church would calm her down. During the offering, the ushers would line up at the back of the church and begin to sing, while marching towards the front of the church. My sisters would be in the line, barely able to move, being that they were so close. It was so funny to me. An educational building had not been built. Therefore, many of the afternoon functions were held in the sanctuary. I remember cakes of all colors— yellow, orange, green, white and purple—stretched across the front of the church. As a young child, I over indulged. To this day, I only eat German Chocolate and Red Velvet cakes.

After the church service was over, it was dinner time. The church had arranged for us to eat at a restaurant called Dee Dex in downtown Charleston, off Meeting Street. We often ordered fried oysters. You could call ahead to place an order. The lady answering the phone would say in her deep Gullah dialect, "yeel lo, D Dax." We also ate at the Ladson House Restaurant. It was very nice. Often there would be a room reserved just for our family. By the way, both of these businesses were Black owned.

Well, when it was time to return to Savannah, there was one stop we had to make before we got home. This made the trip even longer. My sister, Maxine, was attending Mather School in Beaufort, South Carolina. Mather School was founded by Rachel Crane Mather who lived in Boston, Massachusetts. It was started shortly after the Civil War to educate young African-American women. The roads leading to Mather were dark and gloomy as we passed Gardens Corner. Once we arrived at Mather and got Maxine settled, we were off to Savannah's a forty-five minute drive. It's midnight. We are home and there is school tomorrow.

XIII

A WEDDING CONNECTION

A Wedding Connection
1971

On August 7, 1971, Eddie Lamar Jones, Jr. and Maxine Brown Jones were joined in holy matrimony. They exchanged their vows at St. John Baptist Church in Savannah, Georgia. Reverend Matthew Southall Brown, Sr., the bride's father, and Reverend Edward Lamar Ellis, Jr., the bride's uncle, officiated at this sacred ceremony.

Approximately 200 guests were in attendance. Many of the attendees are now deceased. Listed below are some of the guests who signed the registry. I am including theses names in this research because many of these old Savannahnians and out of town guests were and are homeowners. Additionally, the neighborhoods of some of the attendees have gone through tremendous changes. These changes have been both negative and positive.

Historic District
Mrs. Cornelius Sams
Mr. and Mrs, Caleb Bias

Cuyler-Brownville Community
Mr. and Mrs. George May
Mrs. M. E. Eberhardt
Mrs. Nancy H. Walker
Mrs. Isabell Hudson
Mr. Charles Allen
Mrs. Richard Williams

Thunderbolt
Mrs. Marion Butler
Mrs. Marie Kelson
Mrs. Marilyn Butler

Liberty City
Mrs. Clara Bryant
Mrs. Diana Paige

South Carolina
Mr. and Mrs. Walter Jenkins

Cann Park Community

Mrs. Josephine Brown
Miss. Laura Densler
Mr. Henry Sexton
Mrs. Althea James
Mr. and Mrs. E. Leonard Pate
Mrs. Vivian Bradham
Rev. and Mrs. W. N. Robinson
Mr. and Mrs. Benjamin Black

Derrick's Inn

Mrs. Joseph Derrick
Mrs. Laura Derrick Webb
Mrs. Carl Herring

XIV

BIBLIOGRAPHY

Burton, NeSenga   The Root "Montgomery, Alabama
www.Root.com   Razing Homes of African Americans
                         Along the Civil Rights Trail"
                         Sept. 18, 2010, visited 17, Sept. 2010

City-Data.com   Internet visited January-June, 2010
www.City-Data.com

Johnson, Ralph   "Keeping Our Eyes on the Prize: The African
American Preservation Alliance"
        pp. 12 & 13, Homes of Color vol. 6 Issue 1
        January-February-March 2007

New York Post   "Rosa Park's Detroit Home Is Now in Berlin"
        Associated Press, April 7, 2017

Robinson, Eugene   Disintegration: The Splintering of Black, America
        Doubleday, 2010

Schweninger, Loren   Black Property Owners in the South, 1790-1915
                         University of Illinois Press, 1990

Tucker, Stephen   Beyond Atlanta: The Struggle for Racial Equality in
Georgia 1940-1980   University of Georgia Press, 2001

XV

APPENDICES

LISTING OF APPENDICES

1.   State Parent of the Year

2.   Achievers from the Communities

3.   Past and Present Communities

4.   Watch Night

5.   The Ellis Family, 2001

6.   Book Signing

7.   The Derrick Family

8.   Family Accolades

9.   Ministers of the Family and Senior Members of the Family

10.   Boys Summit

11.   "We Speak Your Name" – Lauretta Williams Jones

12.   The Guest Registry-1971

13.   Nyla Jones' Interview With Her Great Grandfather

State Parent of the Year

Some of the Achievers from the Communities

NAMES	COMMUNITIES	ACCOMPLISHMENTS
Lester Anthony	Brownsville	Business Owner / Florist
Harriet Bias Insignares (D)	East Savannah	Faculty, Tennessee State University
Joseph Bias	East Savannah	Minister of Music, Tulsa First United Methodist
Leonard Brown	Cann Park	Systemwide Teacher of the Year, Dekalb County Schools
Matthew S. Brown, Jr.	Cann Park	Minister, First Union Baptist Church
Vernon Bryant	Liberty City	Physician
Frank Bynes	Downtown Savannah	Physician
Marie Crawford	Brownsville	Ph.D., Ohio State University
Walter Gaskins	Liberty City	Lieutenant General, U.S. Marine Corp (NATO)
Paulette B. Green (D)	East Savannah	Faculty, Voorhees College
Herbert Hamilton (D)	Cann Park	City Government; Miami, Florida
Ava Herring (Wokoma)	Derrick's Inn	Ph.D., University of MN
Harry James	Cann Park	Attorney / Judge
Marcelite D. Johnson	Liberty City	Faculty; Tennessee State University
Melvin Johnson, Jr.	Cann Park	Former President, Tennessee State University
Maxine B. Jones	Cann Park	Faculty; Tennessee State University
Altheria Maynard	Cann Park	Director of Nutrition; Chatham County Schools
Joseph Miller (D)	Derrick's Inn	Vice President; Citibank New York
Harold Nevels	Cann Park	Physician
Brenda Roberts	West Savannah	Author, Educator
Christa Brown Stephens (D)	Cann Park	Teacher / Leader; Ph.D. Candidate
Wanda Walker	Brownsville	Journalist
Charles Williams	Cann Park	Pharmacist
Pamela Williams (D)	Cann Park	Physician

D = Deceased

Past and Present African-American Communities

African Americans had and still have a major presence in Savannah, Chatham County, Georgia. Listed below are some of the many communities African Americans inhabited. In these communities, families established firm religious, cultural, and social roots. Today, the influences and legacies of foundational families can be felt and seen in many of these communities.

1. Bayview
2. Beach Institute Neighborhood
3. Burroughs
4. Canebrake
5. Cann Park
6. Carver Village
7. Clearview
8. Cloverdale
9. Coffee Bluff
10. Curry Town
11. Cuyler-Brownville (Brownsville
12. Derrick's Inn
13. Dodge City
14. Frog Town
15. Green Square
16. Green Ward
17. Grimble Point (Dutch Town)
18. Hazard County
19. Hudson Hill
20. LaPageville
21. Liberty City
22. Montgomery
23. Ogeecheeton
24. Old Fort
25. Pin Point
26. Richfield
27. Rossingnol Hill
28. Sand Fly
29. Southover
30. Sun Valley
31. Tatemville
32. Tremont Park
33. Village of St. Gall
34. Waterworks (Springfield Terrance)
35. White Bluff
36. Woodsville-Tompkins
37. Yamacraw

The History of Watch Night in the Black Community

Many of us who live in or grew up in **Black communities** in the United States have heard of Watch Night Service, "the gathering of the faithful in church on New Year's Eve." The service usually begins somewhere from 7:00 p.m. to 10:00 p.m. and ends at midnight and beyond the entrance of the New Year. We have always assumed that Watch Night was a fairly standard Christian religious service—made a bit more Afro-centric because that is what happened when elements of Christianity become linked with the Black Church.

However, there is a reason for the importance of the New Year's Eve service in African-American congregations. The Watch Night Service in **Black communities** that we celebrate today can be traced back to a gathering on December 31, 1862, also known as "Freedom Eve."

On that night, Black people (slave and freedman) came together in churches and private homes, all across the nation, to 'watch for freedom,' anxiously awaiting the news that the Emancipation Proclamation actually had become law. Then, at the stroke of midnight, it was January 1, 1863, and all slaves in the Confederate States were declared legally free. When the news was received, there were prayers, shouts and songs of joy as people fell to their knees and thanked God for their freedom. The day was called Emancipation Proclamation Day or Jubilee Day.

Black people have gathered in churches annually on New Year's Eve ever since—to praise God for bringing us safely through another year. It has been nearly 140 years since the first "Freedom Eve" and many of us were never taught in African-American history about Watch Night, but tradition still brings us together at this time every year to celebrate 'how we got over.'

New Year's Day is not only the beginning of a new year, but also the day that ALL slaves were officially declared free, even though some did not learn of the Emancipation Proclamation until years later. Many churches and organizations, such as the National Association for the Advancement of Colored People (NAACP), celebrate Emancipation Day as the day of freedom for all African Americans.

118.

Taken from: Providence Missionary Baptist Church
              Watch Night Worship Service
              Friday, December 31, 2010

The Ellis Family, 2001

Dear Family and Friends,

This is the season that we wish all, "Peace on Earth and Goodwill to Men." The tragedies of Sept 11, 2001 at the World Trade Center, the Pentagon and in an open field in Pennsylvania, possibly saving the White House, amplifies our wish to the world.

Our country has been changed forever, but there is "Good News" for America. Out of the ashes of these tragedies has sprung a phoenix of love, compassion, and brotherhood for all people of our country. Although we do not know how all this will play out in the end, we know one thing for sure, that ultimately God is in control!

As the celebration of the advent of the birth of Jesus brings joy to the earth, we too rejoice in expectation of the coming of our third grandchild. Sharon and Eddie are expecting. We do not know what Sharon is having but the expected month is June 14, 2002. Sharon and Eddie have experienced numerous blessings this year. In January they moved to Martinez, Ga. (Augusta area). Eddie went into business for himself and is now an agent at State Farm. At State Farm Eddie has been recognized as agent of the year for the state of Ga., and is ranked number sixty-six in the nation. Sharon has a new job with the Labor Department as a service specialist; they both are enjoying their beautiful new home and city.

Joia, Richard and Lillian Grace are fine and much involved in their church at GreenForest Baptist in Decatur, Ga. Richard now manages the men's and shoes departments at the new Store Crest Mall in Decatur. Joia is still at Morehouse School of Medicine doing a great job. Lillian Grace, now 3 1/2 yr.'s old, she loves her church and school at Greenforest Baptist and Mc Catep Christian Early Learning Center. She sings in the two/three yr. old choir, loves ballet, computers, Spanish, puzzles, and telling jokes. She has received numerous awards, like student of the month, certificates for scholastics, choir, and good behavior. In November, she recited the welcome for her class's assembly program and Grandparents Day. How Sweet!

Edward, Gina, and Edward IV still love living by the sea in sunny West Palm Beach, Fl. Edward is still the youth minister at Tabernacle Baptist Church where Rev. Dr. Gerald Kisner is pastor. Some of his community involvement's are: Advisory Bd. member, Urban Youth Impact, Citizen Advisory Council City of Palm Beach Community, Leadership West Palm Beach Class of 2001, Service and Health Committee chair for Front Porch Fl.

119.

Volunteer Service committee member, United Way, Pal, Beach Leadership Council member, and Take Stock in Children. Gina is now a full time student at Palm Beach Atlantic College. She is working on a Master of Science Degree in Counciling Psychology, with a concentration in Mental Health, and Marriage and Family Therapy. We are proud to say that she has made a grade of A in all of her courses. She is a consultant for Substance Abuse Education, and will soon become a consultant for Sexual Violence Prevention.

Little Edward is our little prince. He is in Day Care. He is the typical boy. He is finally potty trained! He told his mother that dinosaurs are extinct and gave her a definition for the word. He still loves the drums, piano, and organ. Rugrats are his favorite videos. Little Edward always looks forward to coming to Savannah, Ga., as he says, to go to Chuckie Cheeses, and to ride the carousel at the mall. How sweet!

Sweetheart and I are truly thankful to God four our family. They make us happy and proud. We have been blessed with a great year (inspite of the happenings in our world).

Our church family is a real blessing. The Lord is moving us to another level as Sweetheart teaches, and preaches the word. In the park that faces the church will be a native-American, African-American Memorial Park. It is a project of Leadership Savannah, which involves the Savannah Housing Authority, the City of Savannah, our church, and some community friends. The project will cost $350,000 and should be completed by the spring of 2002. The sculptor chosen for project is Jerome Meadows, of Washington, D.C. He has done a fantastic job!

In March, I had orthroscopic surgery on my right knee. It is doing quite well. One of my activities for December was to sing with the Spelman/Morehouse Chorus in our 75th Reunion Christmas Carol Concert. What a fabulous experience! Lots of memories! It was great to see old friends and acquaintances.

As this year ends, let us pray for each other, and for those who lead our country and world.

Edward and Lillian Ellis
Love and Blessings Always

120.

Reception & Inaugural Book Signing
"The Best of Pastor Matthew Southall Brown, Sr.'s
6:30 a.m. Meditative Thoughts"
Thursday, September 12, 2013
EOA's Aaron L. Buchsbaum Learning Resource Center
5:00 - 7:00 p.m.
Former Georgia State Senator Diana Harvey Johnson, presiding

Program

Welcome   Dr. George N. Williams
                                 Chairman Emeritus, St. John
                                 Baptist Church Board of Deacons

Welcome   Rev. Matthew Southall Brown, Jr.,
                                 Pastor, first Union Missionary Baptist
                                 Church, representing the Brown Family

Greetings & Invocation   Rev. Dr. George P. Lee, III, Pastor
                                 St. John Baptist Church
                                 "The Mighty Fortress"

Greetings   Sponsors

Introduction   Leonard A. Brown, Decatur, GA
of the Author   representing the Brown Family

Author's Remarks   Reverend/Pastor
                                 Matthew Southall Brown, Sr.

Acknowledgements   Rev/Pastor Brown

The Grace, Book Signing,   Minister Connie Williams,
Fellowship and Refreshments   Owner, Connie Will Care Nursing
                                 Services, Host Committee Chair;
                                 and Ms. Harvey Johnson

121.

Title Sponsors

t. John Baptist Church, "The Mighty
Fortress"
Rev. Dr. George P. Lee, III, Pastor

Tate Law Group
Attorney Mark A. Tate, Principal

Bynes – Royall Funeral Home
rs. Frenhye Bynes-Jones, Proprietor

Gold Sponsors

Vernon T. Bryant, MD.
Dr. and Mrs. Vernon T. Bryant

Pat Mathis Construction Company
Ms. Patricia L. Mathis, Owner

The Polote Corporation
r. Benjamin R. Polote, Sr., Chairman

First African Baptist Church
Rev. Thurmond N. Tillman, Pastor

Silver Sponsors

Dr. and Mrs. George N. Williams
Attorney Bonzo C. Reddick
Mrs. Mamie Small Williams
nacle Communications Corporation
Diana Harvey Johnson, President

Escort Committee
The Brown Family

The Host Committee

The Host Committee

Min. Connie Williams, Chair
Mr. John H. Finney
Executive Director, EOA
Mrs. Areatha W. Scott
Mrs. Sandra Polite-Orr
Mrs. Evelyn Fields
Min. Ella Hammond Sims
Dr. Robert L. Gilbert
Mr. Herman L. Riley
Mr. Lester Anthony
Rev. Carolyn L. Dowse
Ms. Kai Walker
Mr. Bobby L. Lockett
Mr. E. Larry McDuffie
Mrs. Elizabeth Taylor
Ms. Barbara Holman
Mrs. Georgia Ferguson, Caterer
Mr. Erick Brack, Musician

Notes

122.

J. W. DERRICK SUFFERS LOSS

Mr. D. W. Derrick, who essays the art of truck-farming in the neighborhood of Thunderbolt, suffered serious losses to his growing crops of early vegetables during the cold snap of a few weeks ago. Mr. Derrick lost something like 10,000 head of cabbages, all about ready for marketing, besides a good crop of carrots. Many of the farmers in this district suffered likewise.

Mr. Derrick has already begun to plant on a large scale.

BROWN—DERRICK

Mrs. L. A. L. Brown announces the marriage of her youngest daughter, Mamie Alvertina to Prof. Joseph W. Derrick of aG. State Ind. College. The ceremony was performed by Rev T. J. Goodall in the presence of a few intermate friends and his family, Wednesday afternoon at eight thirty o'clock

A DAUGHTER

Prof and Mrs. J W Derrick are happy over the birth of a daughter on August 6th. She will be called Mollie Louise.

Ministers of the Gospel in the Family

Reverend Matthew Southall Brown, Sr.
St. John Baptist Church – 35 years
Savannah, Georgia Retired

Reverend Matthew Southall Brown, Jr.
First Union Baptist Church – 15 years
Savannah, Georgia

Reverend Joseph W. Derrick (Deceased)

Reverend Edward Lamar Ellis, Jr.
First Bryan Baptist Church – 26 years
Savannah, Georgia Retired

Reverend Edward Lamar Ellis, III
Mount Peria Baptist Church – 4 months
Ringgold, Georgia

Reverend Shannon O. Smith
First Mount Sinai Baptist Church – 10 years
Savannah, Georgia

Reverend White
Glory Christian Methodist Episcopal Church (Deceased)

Reverend Edward Williams, Jr.   (Deceased)

Reverend Richard M. Williams
First Bryan Baptist Church – 16 years (Deceased)

Living Senior Members of the Family
55 Years and Older
2011

Dorothy S. Brown	Maxine B. Jones
Leonard A. Brown	Joseph R. Miller (D)
Lottie W. Brown (D)	Phillip L. Miller
Rev. Matthew S. Brown, Sr.	Charles Robinson (D)
Rev. Matthew S. Brown, Jr.	Helen F. Scroggins
Albert B. Cameron, Jr.	Herbert Scroggins
Ronald Cameron (D)	Christa B. Stephens (D)
Rev. Edward Ellis, Sr.	Lorraine W. Spruill
Lillian W. Ellis	Laura Webb (D)
Sarah H. Herring	Ava H. Wokoma
Eddie L. Jones, Sr.	Edward Williams, Sr. (D)
Lauretta W. Jones (D)	Michael Williams , Jr.

Generations to Generations

Boys Summit
July 28th -30th 2011

Dear Sir,

This letter comes to thank you for your participation during our 2010 Boys Summit. We want you to know we are still in touch with several of the boys. If you recall on last year we targeted thirty five (35) at risk African American boys. This year we hope to target fifty (50) boys.

The Boys Summit for 2011 will convene on Thursday July 28th through Saturday July 30th. We will follow the same format as last year. We are requesting that you serve again this year as a presenter. If you can and we hope you can serve as a presenter this year please contact Mrs. Dorothy A. Brown at (912) 925-6714 or myself at (912) 236-3173.

Thank you very much for your participation

Sincerely,

M. Southall Brown, Sr.

Pastor Matthew Southall Brown Sr.

We Speak Your Name

"We Speak Your Name" by Pearl Cleage
Adapted for this memorial by Maxine B. Jones

To my aunts, uncle, cousins, brothers, nieces, nephews; to my daddy and especially Byron, Aunt Lillian and Frances.

You are gathered here to memorialize and speak the name of our loved one, _Lauretta Bernette Williams-Jones._

You are present because you are son, sister, nephew, niece, in-law and friend.

Aunt Lauretta inspired each of us to make our mark in the world; to see what we see, be what we be and be better.

We are because she was....We walk in foot prints made deep by her confident strides. She was un-bought, un-bossed and unbeaten.

You are here to **speak her name**, in your heart, mind and in an oral, unified manner.

A lamp unto our feet – {She was an encourager}; a spirit that lit our paths, a life of excellence; an enduring legacy of love; _**Lauretta, We Speak Your Name.**_

Faithful to God in worship and praise – caring deeply for others, striving to have the mind of Christ; _**Lauretta, We Speak Your Name.**_

Lover of family – a giver, protector and kind – always taking a stand when needed_**; Lauretta, We Speak Your Name.**_

Spoke of and held fast to the memories of her loved ones who preceded her in death; "PaPa" and "Mama Williams;" "Ike,"-{Isaac,} "Buck"-{Edward} and "Issi"-{Isadore} however not realizing Lottie and Christa's call home - they are all made a new and rejoice together around God's throne. _**Lauretta, We Speak Your Name.**_

Gifted Home Economics Student – dedicated educator – diligent in her work – mentor to all who would learn; _**Lauretta, We Speak Your Name.**_

Loyal Friend – enjoyed fellowship where ever she went – supportive; _**Lauretta, We Speak Your Name.**_

Politically astute, socially connected, lover of the arts and comedy; loved couture, (dressing as they say _"TO THE NINES,"_ and who can forget her perfume of choice during her younger years, "Evening In Paris." _**Lauretta, We Speak Your Name.**_

Accepting her "lot" in life – she sought support for her condition, stood her ground and took charge of her life as long as she could; _**Lauretta, We Speak Your Name.**_

Loving Byron unconditionally – with all of the love a mother could give; embracing Frances and a new way of life in Florida; _**Lauretta, We Speak Your Name.**_

We heard these words spoken often and with sincerity, from a mother's heart: "Byron, Mommie Loves You—Mommie Loves You Byron."

And -- to all she would say -- _"Continue To Do Well."_ **LAURETTA, – WE -- SPEAK -- YOUR -- NAME!**

The Guest Registry 1971
Maxine Brown Jones and Eddie Lamar Jones, Jr.

These are some of the guest who signed the registry at the wedding of Eddie Lamar Jones, Jr. and Maxine Andrea Brown Jones. Many of the guests were and are longtime homeowners in Savannah, Georgia. One couple's name I would like to highlight is that of Mr. and Mrs. George May. At one point in African American real estate history, in Savannah, Mr. May was known as being one of the wealthiest property owners. His home still stands on West 40th Street as a testament to his resourcefulness.

Date	Name	Address
	Mrs. Martha Singleton	1522 Habersham St
8-7-71	Mr. & Mrs. Henry Sapp	1006 W. 44th St.
	Mrs. Beatrice Sandin	2409 Jefferson St
	Mrs. Elizabeth Holloway	273 B. Hans Q.
	Mrs. Lillie Jones	721 Pine St.
	Mrs. Estella Harvey	507 E. Boltor
	Mrs. Gloria Johnson	808 Carter St.
	Mrs. Mayme Bacon	515 E. Huntingdon
	Mrs. Lena Baker	535 E. Gwinnett St
8-7-71	Mr. & Mrs. George May	628 W. 40th St.
	Mr. & Mrs. Sidney Jones	11 vis W. na ad St
	Mrs. Lera Solomon	Wilmington Island

Nyla Jones' Interview With Her Great Grandfather

Nyla Jones

Mrs. Reardon

English 8, P6

12 January 2017

Mission Viejo, California

Matthew Southall Brown, Sr.

It is not everyday that you get to talk to your great grandfather who had five careers and has been a key part in the American Civil Rights Movement. Matthew Southall Brown is a sharp and knowledgeable ninety-five year old man who lived a very interesting childhood, a productive life, and is still working as a pastor.

Matthew South Brown lived a very interesting childhood. He often remembers spending his summers in South Carolina with his relatives and cousins; also playing with his childhood dog, Sonny. The first elementary school he went to was a Catholic school. which was more regimented, even though he preferred Baptist. On his first day of school, the first thing he saw was the crucifix. Matthew Brown, young and innocent, was terrified. By the time he got home, his mother noticed that he was quiet and very on task getting homework done quickly. When she asked his about this, he responded that when he saw Jesus on the cross, he thought they were going to do that to him. Sometime later, he switched schools. He said that this elementary school was a more relaxed environment. In this elementary school, he remembers going to a one school, where his aunt taught, with a potbelly stove in the center of the room to keep warm. On his way to elementary school he remembers riding in a Model-T Ford and sitting on the rumble seat. His favorite subject in school was always History. Mostly during this class, he interrupted with inquisitive questions. As he was finishing high school it was fun, but he began to become serious, looking forward to his last year in high school. As he finished out high school, he earned awards for debate and attendance. Childhood life was fun and filled with many experiences but the adult life is even more captivating.

Matthew Southall Brown did not go to college right out of high school. Instead, he enrolled in the military. During his time, America was at war, World War II. When he enrolled, African Americans who wanted to be soldiers were discriminated. Over 10,000 young men enrolled but Matthew was one of the 2221 soldiers who were selected. The only problem was that if Africans American colonels and sergeants wanted to be a part of this group, they had to give up their ranks. When the soldiers came back, they didn't receive their ranks back, and even worse, they didn't get any credit for the work they had done. It wasn't until later that they actually got credit for their hard work. Luckily, Matthew, brave and youthful, was one of the few lucky soldiers that got credit for his work. Many did not know about these 2221 brace young men that fought for our country in World War II. After the war, Reverend Brown did go to Georgia State Industrial College for Colored Youth, but did not graduate. In later years, he did seminars at Nashville School of Theology and Princeton University Seminary. I

In August of 1948 when he was twenty-three years old, Matthew got married to his wife Lottie. They were married for 68 years. The couple lived happily in Savannah, Georgia and had two sons and two daughters. Also as an adult, Reverend Brown had five different careers: Diesel Engineering, Postal Worker, Business, Government and most of all Pastoring. As a hobby, he loved to grow flowers, so he helped to organize the Black Men's Garden Club and the Men's Rose Garden Club. As he became an adult, he became more aware of the injustices rendered by the government, so he became a foot soldier or supporter of Reverend Martin Luther King during the Civil Rights Era. His adult life was very productive.

During his later life, Matthew remains very active. Matthew retired in October, 2006 from St. John Baptist Church after 35 years of service. He still works but mostly on a voluntary basis on behalf of children, youth and adults. Some changes that occurred during his adult life were: Congressional and Presidential Elections and the acquiring of more and better rights for people of color. Matthew Southall Brown now has a combination of twenty-six grand and great grandchildren. Reflecting back on his life, he remembered some important events that happened in his life such as: The Civil Rights Movement, the landing on the moon, the downfall of Richard Nixon, the election of Barack Obama and being invited by the House or Representatives in Washington, D.C. to do the opening prayer.

In summary, Matthew Southall Brown has lived a very interesting and productive life and is still involved in his community today. I have learned that being a leader is not always necessarily about being the president; but it's about the things you do as you are living your life. One word of advice that Matthew Southall Brown says is, "If one fails in life, remember failure is not final. You can still get up after failing and always try again. Always aim at the stars but if you aim at the stars you may get to some high mountain tops." This inspires me daily because it shows me that if I aim high and work hard for what I want, I might get there. If I don't , will still have succeeded because I tried my best and still accomplished many things.

Family Accolades

October 28, 2013

Greetings family! Thank you for sharing information for this issue of The Family Accolades. The last issue was sent to you in June. We have had much sorrow in the family due to deaths and illness but our faith in God continue to spirit our hope. We also celebrate our blessings and joys. Keep sharing your good news and any news that may be of interest to the family. Share the accolades with your children.

OUR CHILDREN:

- **Leighana** (GA) 4th Grade: Honor Roll—Continues violin class and will begin piano lessons soon *(Tia McDaniels and Christopher)*
  Leah (GA) Enjoying her first year in "big school" as a kindergarten student

- **Jordyn** (GA) Walking, Running, Talking and POTTIE TRAINED *(Lakeisha Brown)*

- **Matthew** 6th Grade: (GA) Member of a kids acting troupe-He acts, sings and dances. The troupe went to California this summer *(Matthew Southall Brown, III)*

- **Jalen** (GA) 11th Grade: Honor Roll **(Nykea Murvin-Clay)**

- **Alexis** (GA) 3rd Grade: Honor Roll-Top Best Story Writer-Baptized-Jack and Jill Participant, Augusta Chapter *(Eddie and Sharon Bussey)*
  Aniyah (GA) 6th Grade: Honor Roll-Top Reading Award-Choir and Art Club Medals-Graduated from Children's Choir (Church)to Youth Choir-Participant in Jack and Jill

- **Lillian Grace** (GA) 10th Grade:Honor Roll-Attended Camp at Emory University's School of Medicine. The camp focused on the following interests: Human Anatomy and Disease; Biology, Chemistry, Genetics and Physics. She successfully completed a project entitle, "An Allergy to Water: Aquagenic Utlecaria." *(Richard and Joia Dinkins)*

- **Edward** (TN) 10th Grade: Honor Roll-Performed with youth symphony in Chattanooga, TN. *Congratulations! (Edward and Gena Ellis)*
  Samuel (TN) 5th Grade: Honor Roll

- **Zenobia** (NC) Graduated from high school. Congratulations! *(Eva and Victor Washington)*

Family Accolades

Lamar Jones
Helen Scroggins
Christa Stephens
Katea Watson   Maxine, Derico and Friends
Derico Watson
Helen Willis

Everyone may not need a care giver however I have listed all that I am aware of. Please inform me of others.

DEATHS:

Cousin Joe Miller, September 2, 2013. Those of us who had the pleasure of knowing Joe knew him to be gracious and kind, well educated, successful and one who adored his family. He seemed to have friends nationally and internationally and all who have left messages at the Legacy condolence page have fond remembrances of Joe. We pray for Phillip (Joe's brother) and family as they prepare to travel to upstate New York to inter Joe's remains, November 1.

Please send birth and anniversary dates. I can create the list as you send them to me.

 Engagements, Weddings, Anniversaries

Christopher McDaniels and Tia Brown-McDaniels	Wedded June 22nd	
Andre and Zakia Poythress	Engaged (Renewing of Vows-2014)	
Pastor Matthew (Dorothy) Brown, Jr.	June 4th	35 or 36 years
Pastor Matthew (Lottie) Southall Brown, Sr.	August 4th	60+ years
Eddie (Maxine) Jones	August 7th	42years
Edward (Lillian) Ellis	August 11th	50years
Eddie (Nadir) and Nicole Jones	September	13years

 Birthdays

JUNE:
Lauretta Williams-Jones
Leah Danielle Brown
JULY:
Matthew Southall Brown, Jr.
Matthew Southall Brown, IV
Matthew Southall Brown, Sr.
Katea Jheri Jones
Leighanna Rachel Brown-Hobbs
AUGUST:
Lottie Brown
Khalil Jones
Andre Poythress
SEPTEMBER:

NOVEMBER:
Eddie Jones
DECEMBER:
Nicole Jones
Carolyn Murvin-Brown

Family Accolades

Sharon Bussey who completed 25 years of service with the state of Georgia as Supervisor at the GA Departments of Labor

Eddie Bussey who celebrated 12 years of service at State arm Insurance Agency

Katea Jones who was integral in developing the FLEX-PTO employee approach to time off to begin 2014 for Vanderbilt Employees combining vacation, holiday personal and sick time into one FLEX-PTO

Keisha Brown who was hired as a full time professor in the Math Department at Savannah State University

Eddie and Nicole Jones who successfully located to Atlanta, GA after his promotion to Regional Manager for Ford Credit

Dr. Margie Corney with Belinda Pitts who launched a radio talk show, "Inside Women's Health" which can be heard on Tuesdays at 12:45 pm at 100.9 Rejoice Radio Station-The show is based in Chesapeake, VA.

Maxine Jones who is again published-this time with Tennessee State University's Piano Department in the Proficiency Piano Book-having five original copyrighted pieces in the book—Also honored at Life Way Christian Youth Leader's National Conference for work,. leadership and impact on the lives of children through Christian Music and example

General Walter Gaskins retired from the U.S. Marine Corp/NATO.

PRAYER REQUESTS AND PRAISE....

We begin with a praise report: Christa Stephens has completed the Multiple Myeloma medical procedure and treatment. Christa held to her faith, totally relying on Christ and believing He would bring her through this phase in her life without major medical setbacks. She was hospitalized twice due to temperatures but had no other significant issues. Christa maintained her appetite and remained on her feet through the entire process. The medical care was awesome and two weeks ago, she was told she was near the end of her treatment in Atlanta-that the port would be removed soon...it was removed within a few days. Leonard has been a SUPERIOR care giver and as I drove to the clinic during my visits daily with Christa, I marveled at how the Lord brought Leonard back to Atlanta for such a time as this. Relatives in Atlanta have been absolutely wonderful to Christa and you kept a smile on her face and grace in her heart. Christa must adhere to doctors' orders with her medications and office visits. We pray for our sister's continued life blessing and remind her that nothing is impossible with God. He gives us grace to go through life's situations, mercy and peace to endure the outcomes.

We did not receive prayer requests but we are urged to pray for all family members and care givers. I know of the foDllowing family members who have had medical procedures or are dealing with chronic illness:

Mother (Lottie Brown)   Daddy and Pastor Matt Jr and Dorothy Brown, Care Givers
Aunt Laura (Derrick)
Joia Dinkins
Uncle Edward (Ellis)   Aunt Lillian Ellis
Aunt Jeanette (Herring)
Aunt Lauretta (Jones)   Byron Jones

Family Accolades

Khalil (FL) 12th Grade: A/B Honor Roll-Continues interest in Musical Theater and high school choir **(Eddie Lamar and Nicole Jones..Oanya and Christopher)**

Nyla (GA) 4th Grade: Honor Roll-Highest Score on the FCAT State exam for 3rd grade-Soccer Starting Forward-Student of the Month **(Eddie Lamar and Nicole Jones)**

> **Christopher** (GA) 8th Grade: Honor Roll (All A's) and still starring as a junior pro-athlete on the football field *(Andre and Jakia Poythress)*

> **Alphonso** (TN) 7th Grade: Honor Roll-Sixth Grade Class Representative-Sixth Grade Ambassador for Metro Schools-Nominated to National Association of High School Scholars-White Ho use National Congressional Conference for Youth Moved to Saxophone in school band, now playing Oboe. *(Oerico and Katea Watson)*
> **Oerico** (TN) Teething. Crawling, Laughing and Eating like he works
> **Nia** (TN) 3 Yr old Day Care Class: Getting ready for Pre-K-Enrolled in Debbie's dance Studio

> **Samiyah** (GA) 1st Grade: Awarded a scholarship to Emaculate Conception Catholic School and Student of the Month *(Sierra Benning and Calvin Whitley)*

> **Nadejah** (GA) 9th Grade: Graduated from Camp Creek Middle School *(Vincent and Helen Willis)*

> **Cameron** (GA) 4th Grade: Principal's List (Honor Roll)-First Place Winner in the Media Festival for his project "The Piedmont Region of Atlanta." He advanced to the International Media Festival which will be held in November. Congratulations! *(Vernon and Laura-Michelle Woods)*

> **Tyniqua** (GA) 12th Grade: Honor Roll-Senior Class President **(Keith and Tana Walker)**

OUR ADULTS:
Congratulations To:

Pastor Matthew Southall Brown, Sr. who published in first book in a three book series, "The Best of Pastor Matthew Southall Brown Sr.'s 6:30 AM Meditative Thoughts"-Author House Publishing, 7/16/13. Note that the publishing date is also his birth date

Christa Stephens who retired from the Chatham County Board of Education-34 years

Ava Herring who received Doctorate's Degree (Please advise me of info you may want to share related to the degree)

Aunt Lillian and Uncle Edward Ellis who celebrated 50 years of marriage this fall. The celebration was held in Savannah, GA at Historic First Bryan Baptist Church

Mia Cameron who adopted toddler twins this summer, Isaiah and Alishia

SEPTEMBER:
Christa Brown Stephens
Lillian Ellis
Sharon Bussey
Keisha Brown

OCTOBER:
Nyla Jones
Nadir Jones
LaTia Brown McDaniels

December:
Matthew S. Brown III

Notes

Pam,

Know your history better
then those who spick of it.

Leonel Brown
1/13/2019

135.

Made in the USA
Columbia, SC
09 January 2019